HYPOTHERMIA
FROSTBITE AND OTHER
COLD INJURIES

PREVENTION, SURVIVAL, RESCUE, AND TREATMENT

HYPOTHERMIA FROSTBITE AND OTHER COLD INJURIES

PREVENTION, SURVIVAL, RESCUE, AND TREATMENT

SECOND EDITION

Gordon G. Giesbrecht, Ph.D.
James A. Wilkerson, M.D.

With the Assistance of
Andrea R. Gravatt, M.D.
Murray P. Hamlet, D.V.M.
Frank R. Hubbell, D.O.

THE MOUNTAINEERS BOOKS

THE MOUNTAINEERS BOOKS
*is the nonprofit publishing arm of The Mountaineers Club,
an organization founded in 1906 and dedicated to the exploration,
preservation, and enjoyment of outdoor and wilderness areas.*

1001 SW Klickitat Way, Suite 201, Seattle, WA 98134

First edition, 1986. Second edition, 2006.

Manufactured in the United States of America

Project Editor: Mary Metz
Copy Editor: Cindy Bohn
Cover, book design: Peggy Egerdahl
Layout: Kristy W. Thompson
Illustrator: Brian Metz

Cover photograph: *Thermometer outside in the snow.* © Royalty-Free/Corbis

Library of Congress Cataloging-in-Publication Data
Hypothermia, frostbite, and other cold injuries : prevention, survival, rescue
and treatment / Gordon G. Giesbrecht . . . [et al.]. — 2nd ed.
    p. cm.
  Includes index.
  ISBN 0-89886-892-0
  1. Hypothermia. 2. Frostbite. 3. First aid in illness and injury. I. Giesbrecht,
Gordon G.
  RC88.5.H964 2006
  616.9'89—dc22
                                2006008885

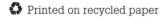 Printed on recycled paper

CONTENTS

AN APPRECIATION

THE WRITERS WOULD LIKE TO RECOGNIZE a trio of investigators, now retired, who devoted much of their careers to exploring cold injuries and developing techniques for treating them.

William J. Mills, Sr., M.D., an orthopedist in Anchorage, Alaska, almost single-handedly changed the standard of care for treatment of frostbite from slow thawing to rapid rewarming in warm water. This practice greatly improves prognosis and has undoubtedly saved many limbs from amputation, no small accomplishment when the accepted standard of care for frostbite for most of the past two hundred years was to actively cool frostbitten tissue.

Murray P. Hamlet, D.V.M., the former director of the Cold Research Laboratory at the U.S. Army Research Institute of Environmental Medicine in Natick, Massachusetts, is an authority on all cold injuries, particularly their prevention. Not only is he a coauthor of Chapter Ten, "Cold Weather Clothing," but through his investigations and many educational programs, particularly his informative and entertaining lectures, Murray has been the source for much of the information in the other chapters.

Gerald K. Bristow, M.D., an anesthesiologist and emergency medicine physician in Winnipeg, Manitoba, is renowned in Canada for his expertise in the clinical treatment of severely hypothermic patients. The most important professional event in the career of one of the authors of this book occurred when Gerald agreed to provide medical supervision for human hypothermia studies for Gordon's master's thesis. A research partnership developed and still continues after twenty years! Thanks, Gerald, for making such research, much of which is quoted in this book, possible.

INTRODUCTION

ON A BEAUTIFUL WINTER DAY in February 1990, twenty-two teens and counselors from a private camp for youths on probation were walking on Convict Lake in the Sierra Nevada Mountains when a tragedy occurred. Four boys ventured farther out on the ice than they should have and, one by one, broke through and began frantically screaming. One of the boys managed to escape the water's icy grip. Two counselors approached the scene to assist but quickly fell through also. Help was summoned and emergency medical service personnel arrived within minutes. Without delay a member of the U.S. Forest Service moved onto the ice to perform a rescue only to be added to the chaotic mass of panicked "swimmers." Unbelievably, two more rescue professionals—volunteer firefighters—followed and also broke through. It was not until better-equipped rescue personnel arrived that a safe rescue attempt could be made . . . on one lone adult. In just fifteen minutes, three boys and four of their five adult rescuers were dead.

The *Los Angeles Times* headlined a front page article, "7 Apparently Drown in Freezing Sierra Lake Tragedy." Many rescue and medical professionals, as well as the general public, believed the victims succumbed to hypothermia. But hypothermia did not kill anyone. The condition of the lone survivor provided great insight into what happened to the victims. Rescuers noticed that when they approached him, he was hyperventilating intensely and beginning to lose consciousness. Medical personnel who examined the man described him as ataxic (clumsy), severely alkalotic (a sign of prolonged hyperventilation), and numb. However, on arrival at a hospital, the survivor had a normal body temperature. In fact, all seven casualties would have been normothermic when they found their icy grave.

What killed them if not hypothermia? In 1990, few people, medical and rescue personnel included, understood that the first two responses to cold water immersion—cold shock and cold incapacitation—long precede the onset of hypothermia. The initial response to sudden immersion in cold water is gasping and rapid breathing, an effect that usually disappears within thirty seconds to a few minutes. Yet the single survivor was still hyperventilating after ten to fifteen minutes of immersion. Panic is known to prolong initial cold shock. In fact, many (or all) of the victims probably panicked to some extent—and then drowned—either from aspirating water during uncontrolled breathing or after being incapacitated by thrashing about in the cold water. Either of these actions could lead to drowning within as little as a minute or two.

The real tragedy is that all seven of these individuals could probably have survived the fifteen minutes in icy water if they had been able to get their breathing under control and merely placed their arms on the ice and stopped struggling. Such knowledge is essential for victims who need to increase their chances for rescue. It is also essential information for rescue personnel. Understanding that victims can last longer than usually believed would allow them to plan safer, more successful rescue strategies, while preventing rescuers from rushing in and becoming secondary victims themselves.

Understanding how the body reacts to cold, what causes cold injuries, and how to prevent and treat these injuries is essential for winter-sport participants. Individuals must know their clothing: specifically what to buy and how to use it. Cold weather enthusiasts should also be familiar with cold water rescue techniques (either for themselves or others) and be prepared to survive when an adverse event has left them wet, cold, without much of their equipment, and possibly injured.

Information and repeated practice must be combined. Armed with these tools, individuals can step outside the box—outside their comfort zone—and experience many exciting and fulfilling winter activities. They can prepare properly, preventing adverse cold exposure, but they can also build confidence in their ability to deal competently with reasonable worst-case scenarios.

This book is being revised after twenty years because the understanding of cold and cold injuries has changed, and updated information is needed by individuals ranging from medical and rescue personnel to the general public. Not only is much of the information in this second edition new, but the writers have tried to present it in a way that makes complex concepts easy to understand, remember, and apply. They have tried to make cold physiology easier to comprehend and to provide a new approach to understanding hypothermia; how to recognize the condition and how best to treat it. The discussion of cold weather clothing has been updated to include new products, and a new, more accurate wind-chill chart developed by Canadian authorities has been included. Four new chapters have been added. "Cold Water Drowning" includes consideration of the events that enable individuals to survive neurologically intact an hour or more of submersion in cold water. "Other Nonfreezing Cold

Injuries" considers chilblains and pernio in more detail and contains entirely new discussions of Raynaud's phenomenon, cold panniculitis, cold-induced urticaria, breathing in the cold and cold-induced asthma, and cold-induced vasomotor rhinitis. A new chapter on survival describes techniques for getting through an unexpected stranding in cold, wilderness environments unharmed. A final chapter describes safe practices for working on the ice and ice-water escape and rescue techniques that would be useful to the general public and to professionals, particularly individuals living in Canada, the northern United States, and northern European countries.

A NOTE ABOUT SAFETY

Safety is an important concern in all outdoor activities. No book can alert you to every hazard or anticipate the limitations of every reader. The descriptions of techniques and procedures in this book are intended to provide general information. This is not a complete text on cold injuries. Nothing substitutes for formal instruction, routine practice, and plenty of experience. When you follow any of the procedures described here, you assume responsibility for your own safety. Use this book as a general guide to further information.

The Mountaineers Books

CHAPTER 1

Baby It's Cold Outside:
Basic Human Cold Physiology

THE HUMAN BODY is considered homeothermic (Greek *homos*: the same; *therme*: heat) because it maintains a near-constant, average core temperature of 98.6° F (37° C) in the face of environmental extremes. (The term *core* refers to the internal organs, primarily the heart, lungs, liver, and brain.) Humans are warm-blooded mammals and are classified as endothermic (Greek *endo*: within) because most of the heat that maintains this constant temperature is produced within the body by metabolic functions, which can be augmented by muscular activity. In contrast, cold-blooded animals, such as reptiles and fish, have a body temperature that varies considerably; they are considered exothermic (Greek *exo*: without) because much of their body heat is derived from their environment.

A person's core temperature usually varies throughout the day by 1.25° to 3.75° F (0.7° to 2.1° C) with the lowest values occurring in the early morning—3:00 AM to 5:00 AM—and highest values in the late afternoon or early evening for individuals who are awake during the day. The average variation is 2.7° F (1.5° C) for men and 2.2° F (1.2° C) for women. Additionally, women's core temperatures vary with their menstrual cycles, rising about 1.0° F (0.5° C) at the time of ovulation and staying at that level until menstruation begins.

During prolonged vigorous exercise, such as competitive distance running, a healthy person's temperature can increase dramatically because heat is being produced faster than it can be lost. When vigorous, continuous exercise occurs in hot, humid conditions, core temperatures as high as 104° F (40° C) are not uncommon. High humidity impairs heat dissipation because it slows evaporation of perspiration, and increasing core temperatures can lead to heat illnesses and eventually heatstroke. On the other hand, exposure to cold can result in local cold injuries, such as frostbite, or a more global decrease in body core temperature known as hypothermia.

HUMAN THERMOREGULATORY CONTROL

Core temperature ultimately depends on the balance between heat gain and heat loss (Figure 1-1). When the body is resting, metabolic biochemical reactions

HEAT GAIN	HEAT LOSS
Resting metabolism	Sweating (↑ evaporation)
(heat production)	Vasodilation (↑ radiation)
Shivering (↑ production)	Vasoconstriction (↓radiation)
Exercise (↑ production)	Insulation/Vapor barrier
External heat (↑ donation)	(↓ conduction)
External cooling (removal)	(↓ convection)

Figure 1-1. Core temperature depends on the balance between heat gain and heat loss. Features above the dashed lines are physiological mechanisms; features below the dashed lines are environmental conditions.

in the muscles and organs, predominantly the liver, produce about 1,000 calories (one kilocalorie) of heat per kilogram of body weight per hour. Most of this heat (90 to 95 percent) is removed by circulating blood and dissipated through the skin, although smaller amounts are lost through the lungs. In calm air at temperatures between about 82° and 93° F (28° and 34° C), the air is warm enough to pose no threat of chilling a nude adult human body and is cool enough to absorb the heat produced by the body—heat that under warmer conditions would require metabolic work, such as sweating, to aid in its loss. Under these conditions heat gain is passively balanced with heat loss, and this range of air temperatures has been labeled the thermoneutral zone.

Humans are able to maintain an almost constant core temperature in spite of considerable swings in the temperature of the environment. This control is achieved in two ways: through involuntary physiologic responses that increase or decrease heat loss and heat gain and by deliberate voluntary actions that provide greater protection from heat or cold than physiologic responses alone.

The involuntary mechanisms that determine heat loss and heat production are regulated—turned on and off and finely balanced—in two ways. In mammals, the dominant control is exerted by the temperature control center located in an area at the base of the brain known as the hypothalamus. However, blood vessels in the skin are capable of reacting to temperature changes even when the nerves connecting them with the brain have been cut, so cutaneous control mechanisms must also exist.

The temperature control center functions much like a thermostat and responds to information received from two sources: the temperature of the blood that bathes the brain and other central structures and impulses from thermosensitive receptors in the skin (Figure 1-2). The information from these two sources provides an integrated thermal signal, which is compared with a target (setpoint) temperature, usually normal body temperature. If the integrated thermal signal is above the setpoint, cooling responses are initiated, including heat avoidance behavior, vasodilation, and sweating. If the signal is below the setpoint, warming responses are initiated, including cold avoidance behavior, vasoconstriction, and shivering.

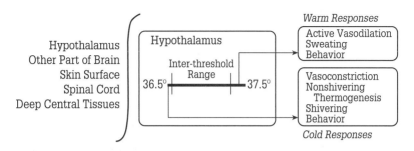

Figure 1-2. Schematic diagram of thermoregulatory control. Temperature inputs are received from skin and core structures and are integrated in the hypothalamus. Depending on whether the integrated thermal signal is above or below the setpoint (36.5°–37.5° C), warm or cold responses are initiated.

The posterior portion of the hypothalamic thermoregulatory center controls heat retention by decreasing heat loss and increasing heat production. If this portion of the center is destroyed, an animal cannot conserve heat when it is in a cold environment but loses heat normally when it is warmed. The anterior portion of the center has opposite functions and is known as the heat loss center. If this portion of the brain is destroyed, an animal can maintain its temperature in a cold environment but cannot lose heat in a hot environment.

The integrated thermal signal can stimulate a response even if only one source of thermal information changes. For example, an immobile person immersed in cold water begins to shiver as skin temperature falls, even though core temperature—and therefore the temperature of the blood circulating through the brain—is still normal. If this person remains in water that is cold enough, core temperature eventually falls in spite of the shivering. If he is subsequently removed from the cold water and placed in a warm bath, shivering stops as soon as the skin becomes warm, even though core temperature may still be falling.

Each thermoregulatory response—vasodilation, sweating, vasoconstriction, and shivering—can be characterized by its threshold and gain. The threshold is the value of the integrated signal at which the response is initiated; the gain is the change in intensity of the response with changes in the integrated thermal signal. Thermal responses follow a general pattern. As the thermal signal increases, vasodilation is initiated before sweating because the threshold for vasodilation is reached before the threshold for sweating, and both responses increase in intensity as the thermal signal continues to increase. Likewise, as the thermal signal decreases below the setpoint, vasoconstriction is initiated before shivering because the threshold for vasoconstriciton is reached first, and both responses increase in intensity as the thermal signal continues to decrease.

CONTROL OF BLOOD FLOW

Aside from behavioral changes, the body generally changes blood flow first because this requires less energy than shivering or sweating. In cold conditions, physiologic regulation of body temperature depends mainly upon decreased cutaneous heat loss (through peripheral vasoconstriction) and increased heat production (through shivering and exercise). Vascular constriction and dilation in the fingers and toes can change blood flow one hundredfold, from 80–90 cc/min/100 cc tissue during full dilation, to 0.5–1.0 cc/min/100 cc tissue during full constriction. This decreased blood flow reduces heat input into, and therefore heat loss from, the limbs. Most blood flow control occurs in the hands and feet and is regulated through arteriovenous anastomoses (AVAs), which are more concentrated in the tips of the fingers and toes. Figure 1-3 shows the high concentration of small blood vessels in the fingertips.

Figure 1-3. Blood vessels of the wrist and hand. The number of small vessels increases at the fingertips.

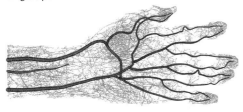

In general, the capillary bed provides nutritive blood flow and the arteriovenous anastomoses (AVAs) regulate thermoregulatory blood flow (Figure 1-4). Capillary flow is dependant on the metabolic requirements of the tissues, which vary with the amount of work being done (generally minimal in the fingertips) and the tissue temperature (as tissue temperature decreases, metabolism and capillary blood flow decrease). AVA flow is essentially for thermoregulatory control and provides a direct conduit between the arterial and venous blood vessels. Opening the AVAs (vasodilation) greatly increases flow through fingers and

Figure 1-4. Schematic drawing of the microvasculature in the fingertip. The cutaneous capillary bed provides nutritive blood flow to the tissues. The arteriovenous anastomoses (AVAs) are comparatively large connections between arterial and venous vessels; their main function is to regulate blood flow through the fingertips, and therefore through the arm.

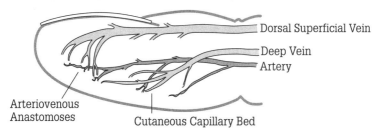

Dorsal Superficial Vein

Deep Vein

Artery

Arteriovenous Anastomoses

Cutaneous Capillary Bed

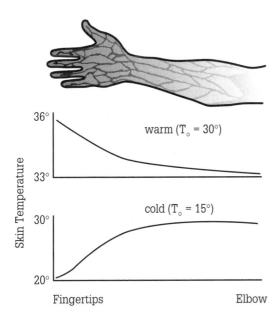

Figure 1-5. Skin temperature increases from the elbow to fingertips in warm conditions where arteriovenous anastomoses (AVAs) are open (vasodilation). In cold conditions, AVAs close (vasoconstriction), and skin temperature decreases from the elbow to fingertips.

toes, and thus entire limbs, which increases heat delivery to, and loss from, the periphery. Figure 1-5 illustrates a surprising phenomenon. In a warm human, the fingertips are the warmest part of the limb and skin temperature decreases as the venous blood returns along the surface veins of the forearm. (Similar phenomena occur in the leg.) Conversely, when a human is cold, the AVAs close (vasoconstrict), peripheral blood flow is virtually eliminated, and skin temperature decreases from the elbow towards the fingertips (and knee to toes). Heat delivery and heat loss in the limb are decreased and the core temperature is protected.

Thermoregulatory blood flow through the limbs to the periphery is regulated mainly through the tips of the fingers and toes and is controlled by central thermoregulatory mechanisms. However, local cooling or warming can also influence flow rates in these areas.

The value of vasoconstriction is the prevention of body core cooling by decreasing heat loss from the periphery. Of course, decreased blood flow, and therefore heat delivery, to the hands and feet allows pronounced cooling, which decreases the ability to perform physical tasks and increases the risk of freezing the tissue (frostbite).

CONTROL OF HEAT PRODUCTION

If vasoconstriction, and its consequent decrease in heat loss, is not enough to protect thermal homeostasis, an increase in heat production may be necessary. The only effective way adult humans can increase heat production is by increasing muscular activity. Metabolic heat production in other tissues may be increased briefly by the hormones epinephrine and norepinephrine (adrenaline and noradrenaline), or over a longer period of time by increases in thyroid hormones, but the quantity of heat produced is insignificant in comparison with the quantities required to warm the entire body.

To significantly increase heat production the body involuntarily resorts to shivering. Shivering is merely inefficient exercise, consisting of alternating muscle contraction and relaxation. About 80 percent of the consumed energy is given off as heat. Heat production during shivering can be as much as five times greater than heat production at rest. The purpose of this increased heat production is to prevent, or at least delay, the onset of hypothermia.

Shivering is initiated and controlled by a decreased integrated thermal signal. In fact, decreased skin temperature alone generally initiates shivering before core temperature decreases. Therefore, initial shivering is usually not a sign of hypothermia, but is an initial sign of cold stress and should be taken as a warning that hypothermia may occur if nothing is done to improve the situation. The heating power of shivering is illustrated in Figure 1-6. In this example, shivering heat production actually increases core temperature in 50° F (10° C) air, halts the decrease in core temperature in 59° F (15° C) water, and slows the onset of hypothermia in 46.4° F (8° C) water.

Since shivering is generally an initial warning that heat balance is being threatened, in the early stages of cold stress an individual might be better off performing useful work, such as hiking out of a threatening situation or preparing a campsite and gathering firewood. This muscular exercise produces a considerable amount of heat and is more productive and comfortable than shivering.

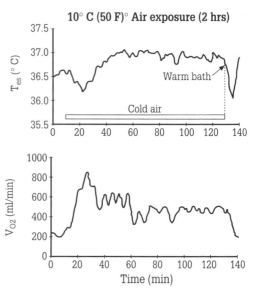

Figure 1-6. Shivering heat production (SHP) (indicated by Vo₂ in bottom panels) and core temperature (indicated by T_{es} in top panels) in three cold stress conditions. In 50° F (10° C) air, SHP is about two and a half times resting metabolic heat production and maintains body core temperature above precooling levels.

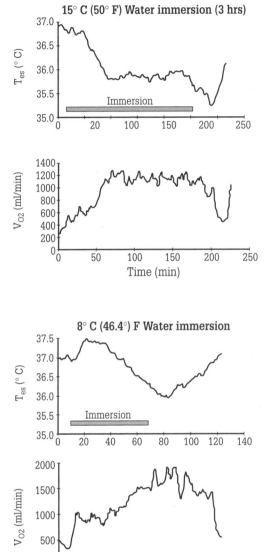

15° C (50° F) Water immersion (3 hrs)

Immersion

8° C (46.4°) F Water immersion

Immersion

During immersion in 59° F (15° C) water, SHP increases in response to decreased core temperature and plateaus at a level five times above resting metabolic rate, which prevents any further drop in core temperature over the next two hours of immersion. In an extreme cold stress (immersion in 46.4° F [8° C] water), SHP increases continuously in response to decreased core temperature but is not able to prevent core cooling. However, core temperature would have decreased at a much faster rate if shivering was absent.

If hypothermia develops and continues to worsen, thermoregulatory control fails, and shivering eventually stops when core temperature falls below about 90° F (32° C). Alcohol, tranquilizers, opioids, low blood sugar, and high altitude tend to inhibit shivering. Ingestion of such drugs, exercising to exhaustion, or altitude hypoxia predispose an individual to hypothermia by inhibiting shivering as well as by impairing intellectual function.

VOLUNTARY RESPONSES TO THERMAL STRESS

Humans normally take action in response to the sensation of warm or cool skin. These actions include avoidance, changing the surrounding microenvironment, or changing activity levels. In response to a warm environment, a person can seek shade, take off clothing, stop exercising, or pour water over the skin and clothing to promote evaporative cooling. An individual can respond to cold by engaging in voluntary physical activity, wearing protective clothing, constructing shelters, and manipulating sources of heat such as fire.

PHYSICAL FACTORS AFFECTING THE RATE OF BODY CORE COOLING

Several physical factors have a significant effect on the rate of heat loss and body core cooling. Obviously, the ambient temperature directly affects heat loss. The medium to which a person is exposed is also important. For instance, water has higher thermal conductivity than air. Water conducts heat away from the body approximately twenty-five times faster than air at the same temperature. This explains why water that is the same temperature as a typical room (70° F or 21° C) feels much colder.

Body morphology (composition and size) also greatly influences heat loss. Fat is an insulator, and the one time being obese is beneficial is during cold stress. Individuals with more body fat generally cool at a slower rate than their thinner friends.

Because most heat is lost through the skin, the ratio of the area of the skin surface to the volume of the body determines the speed with which heat is lost. Small bodies have a significantly larger surface-to-volume ratio than large bodies. The differences in these ratios can be illustrated with cubes measuring one inch and two inches on each side. The one-inch cube has a volume of one cubic inch (1 in. x 1 in. x 1 in.), a surface of six square inches (1 in. x 1 in. x 6 = 6), and a surface-to-volume ratio of 6:1. The larger two-inch cube has a volume of eight cubic inches (2 in. x 2 in. x 2 in.), and a surface of twenty-four square inches (2 in. x 2 in. x 6 = 24), but a surface-to-volume ratio of only 3:1. Heat would be lost much faster from the smaller cube.

As a result of the proportionally greater surface area of their skin, babies, children, and even small adults can lose heat considerably faster than larger individuals in identical situations. Heat is lost faster from the extremities than from the trunk because the cylinders that make up the extremities (fingers and limbs) have a proportionately greater surface area than the trunk cylinder.

ADAPTATION TO COLD

Certain peoples have an incredible tolerance for cold. Resting body metabolism rates and the secretion of thyroid hormones are mildly increased in inhabitants of cold climates, but not enough to be protective. Investigation has shown that humans respond to repeated, or long-term, cold exposure in a way that is specific to their type of exposure. In general, humans adapt to cold by a process of accommodation—developing a decreased response to the same stimulus or stress. Charles Darwin described women of Tierra del Fuego who suffered no apparent discomfort nursing their babies in open boats while snow fell on their bare breasts. The aboriginals of central Australia, who are renowned for their cold tolerance, can remain asleep at cold nighttime air temperatures after their core temperature has begun to fall, which allows them to sleep on the cold ground while conserving energy by not shivering. Nonacclimated individuals almost inevitably wake up when their core temperature drops.

Most people experience cold stress to their hands and feet when exposed to cold while being somewhat underdressed for the weather. The normal physiologic response to this type of cold stress would be decreased blood flow, and therefore decreased heat delivery, to the hands and feet; pronounced cooling and a decreased ability to perform physical tasks; and an increased risk of freezing the tissue. Experiencing significant vasoconstriction in the cold may not be beneficial if a person makes a living, or is required to survive, in the cold.

Figure 1-7 illustrates the differences in fingertip temperature between two subjects: one was cold-acclimated over many generations (Inuit) and the other was nonacclimated (Caucasian). The cold-acclimated Inuit man has developed a different physiologic strategy for dealing with cold exposure. He needs to use his hands for long periods in the cold. Therefore his thermoregulatory control has shifted to allow more blood flow to the periphery. In all warm and cold conditions, his peripheral blood flow is higher and his skin is warmer. This allows him to keep his fingertips warmer and to work longer, more safely, and more efficiently in the cold. Additionally, even when exposed to -4° F (-20° C), he experiences transient increases in skin temperature during brief periods of vasodilation. This cold-induced vasodilation (CIVD), known as the Lewis hunting response, provides further protection against tissue freezing and prolongs work time in the cold. This phenomenon partially explains why cold water fishermen, Lapps, Eskimos, and similar people can work with bare hands for long periods of time in conditions most others find intolerable.

Although long-term residents of cold environments have developed their adaptation to the cold over generations, any individual experiences a similar, though smaller, response after repeated cold exposure. In fact, most people have experienced warmer-feeling hands within days, or even hours, of cold

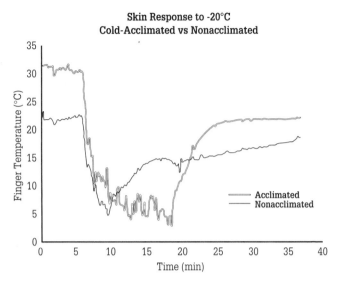

Figure 1-7. Skin temperature responses of cold-acclimated and nonacclimated subjects. Acclimated individuals have much warmer skin in a warm environment and during exposure to -4° F (-20° C). They also warm up much quicker after exiting the cold, even though they were exposed to the cold for a longer period. (The transient increases in skin temperature during cold exposure are examples of cold-induced vasodilation, also known as the Lewis hunting response.)

exposure, which marks the beginning of the continuum of cold adaptation.

A final word on adaptation relates to brown adipose tissue. All newborn placental mammals, including human infants, have deposits of fatty tissue known as brown fat. Within the cells of this tissue, fat is stored as multiple small droplets instead of one large globule, as in ordinary fat cells. Brown fat cells also contain numerous large mitochondria, the energy producing structures of all cells. Unlike ordinary fat cells that can only store fat, these cells are capable of metabolizing fat in response to hormones such as insulin and epinephrine or in response to sympathetic neural stimulation. In laboratory animals—mostly rats—these cells have been found to play a critical role in producing heat in a cold environment. They also help prevent obesity because they can metabolize fat at a very rapid rate without having to perform some other function, as do muscle cells, for instance.

Large quantities of brown fat are retained into adulthood in all small placental mammals, particularly hibernators. However, in humans brown fat largely disappears shortly after birth and cannot be regenerated in response to cold exposure. Although brown fat plays a major role in temperature regulation in newborn humans, its role at later stages of life is generally considered minimal.

MEASURING BODY TEMPERATURE

Temperature is measured with thermometers, most of which contain a material that either expands or sends out a greater electrical current as it is warmed. Mercury, a metal that is liquid at environmental temperatures, expands in a relatively uniform manner when it is heated. Mercury thermometers are inexpensive, easy to carry, and accurate. However, they require several minutes to register the actual temperature and are made of glass that is easily broken.

Clinical thermometers are mercury thermometers with a valve that inhibits the return of mercury to the bulb and reduces the delay before the actual temperature is indicated. Prior to use, such thermometers must be shaken down to return enough mercury to the bulb for the indicated temperature to be below that being measured. Most clinical thermometers are designed to measure an increase in body temperature—fever or hyperthermia—and only register as low as about 94° F (34.5° C). For situations in which subnormal body temperatures are anticipated thermometers that can measure temperatures as low as 75° to 81° F (24° to 27° C) are necessary.

Electronic thermometers are accurate, easier to read, and register temperature much faster than mercury thermometers. Sterilization is assured either by disposable probes or a discardable sheath over the probe. Electronic thermometers are expensive, too bulky to be routinely carried into wilderness areas, and may not be accurate in the cold, which shortens battery life. An alternate, non-battery-dependent thermometer must be available.

Body temperature can be measured most readily by placing an oral thermometer beneath the tongue (the average body core temperatures cited at the beginning of this chapter are based on oral measurements), although this method is slow and has safety limitations. Mercury thermometers must be left in place for about three minutes with the mouth closed and otherwise empty. Measuring oral temperatures with glass thermometers is unsafe if the individual is not fully conscious and cooperative because the thermometer could be broken by biting and the glass fragments could produce severe injuries.

Axillary (armpit) temperatures are about 1° F (0.5° C) lower than oral temperatures, but can be used when temperature measurements cannot be obtained from other sites because the individual is injured or uncooperative. An oral or rectal thermometer can be placed in the armpit and the arm held against the side of the body for two to three minutes. Axillary temperatures are less reliable because they are so variable. They are not precise enough for early detection of temperature changes in persons with febrile illnesses, but they are accurate enough for evaluating hypothermic individuals in a wilderness setting. Core temperature is roughly 2° F (1° C) higher than the axillary temperature. An axillary temperature of 93° F (34° C) indicates only mild hypothermia.

Esophageal temperature is now considered the best noninvasive measure of heart (core) temperature. A probe is passed through the nose and down the esophagus to the level of the heart. The esophageal measurements virtually mirror the actual heart measurements.

Tympanic membrane (eardrum) temperatures theoretically reflect body core temperature accurately. Infrared thermometers are used in most hospitals, but are unreliable when used in field settings. A special epitympanic device includes a probe within the ear canal and an ear piece that completely insulates the exterior ear. Although this device is commonly used by search and rescue (SAR) groups in Europe, it is not commonly used in North America.

Rectal temperatures are usually about 1° F (0.5° C) higher than oral temperatures and more accurately reflect body core temperatures. However, when a hypothermic individual is being rewarmed, rectal temperatures tend to lag behind core temperatures. Additionally, a rectal thermometer or temperature probe may be inserted into feces, which are much slower to rewarm than the body core, resulting in an inaccurate low temperature reading. A rectal thermometer should be lubricated and inserted two to three inches into the rectum; a lubricated temperature probe can be inserted five to six inches. Due to their inconvenience, and the danger that the movement required to take a rectal temperature would induce ventricular fibrillation in a moderately to severely hypothermic individual, rectal temperatures are rarely measured outside of a medical center.

Within recent years a variety of tapes that change color or otherwise indicate temperature have been developed. These are useful for screening for an elevated temperature, but no such devices are currently available for measuring temperatures in the hypothermic range.

Most groups encountering hypothermia in the wilderness do not rely on thermometers. Decisions concerning an individual's condition and treatment are based on signs and symptoms, not on a measured temperature.

CHAPTER 2

The Cold Hard Facts:
Cold Pathophysiology

PREVENTING, RECOGNIZING, AND TREATING cold injuries requires an understanding of the effects of cooling on the body. All human functions are the results of complex biochemical reactions, and all such reactions require time for completion. That time is always prolonged if the reactants are cooled. Biochemical reactions have an optimal temperature, which for those occurring in humans is normal body temperature. Temperatures that are higher or lower disturb the efficiency of the reactions and the manner in which they mesh with other biochemical reactions. As the body is cooled, all functions become slower and less efficient, although such slowing may not be noticeable until cooling is relatively severe.

Solutions tend to increase in viscosity—thicken—as they are cooled. Like automobile engine oil on a cold morning or cold maple syrup, blood also thickens when cooled. Pliable materials such as plastics become stiff and rigid. Tendons and muscles do also.

The molecules in gases bounce off one another less vigorously when cooled, which allows them to come closer together and occupy a smaller volume and increases their solubility in liquids. The increased solubility of oxygen in the cold blood of the ice fish allows all of the oxygen needed for that animal's metabolism to be carried in solution. The species does not need—and does not have—hemoglobin to carry oxygen.

The body is composed of organ systems that must function effectively if all are to survive. For example, the circulatory system carries nutrients digested and absorbed by the gastrointestinal system to the liver, where they are further modified. The nutrients are then carried to muscles, where they are broken down into water and carbon dioxide as work is performed. The circulatory system carries the excess water to the kidneys, where it is eliminated, and the carbon dioxide to the lungs, where it is exhaled. Cold does not affect all organ systems uniformly. But it can cause one system to fail, which in turn can cause others to fail.

Until the core temperature approaches 90° F (32° C) the body's response to cooling consists mostly of efforts to restore normal temperature. The primary effect of body cooling is a decrease in tissue metabolism and gradual inhibition of neural transmission and control. However, in a body that is intact and conscious, secondary responses to skin cooling predominate. Therefore, sudden cooling of the skin initiates shivering and increases metabolism, ventilation, heart rate, and cardiac output. The primary effects of cooling are seen at lower core temperatures (less than 90° F [32° C]), when shivering ceases and metabolism, ventilation, heart rate, and cardiac output decrease along with the fall in core temperature.

As the body continues to cool, the chemical reactions requiring oxygen slow down, and the metabolic need for oxygen diminishes in proportion to the reduced supply from the lungs and circulatory system. With more severe hypothermia, the changes in function become more abnormal and are often deleterious to the body as a whole. The reduction in oxygen supply is usually greater than the reduction in oxygen demand.

With few exceptions, the physiologic changes that result from rapid cooling by immersion in cold water differ very little from those caused by slower cooling in air. (Water immersion may be complicated by water in the lungs or drowning.) However, the slower cooling in air allows more time for undesirable metabolic changes, which can hinder or totally prevent an individual's recovery.

CHANGES IN SPECIFIC ORGANS
Muscles

Mild cooling directly affects muscle tissue to cause stiffness and incoordination. The amount of oxygen consumed in the performance of simple tasks increases tremendously. Involuntary shivering causes some incoordination that can be overcome by voluntary movement. Profound cooling decreases the rate at which nerve impulses are conducted to the muscles and decreases the response by the muscle tissue. The muscles are unable to contract effectively (weakness), and contracted muscles may be unable to relax (tetany). The result is jerky, uncoordinated movements, staggering, and loss of the ability to perform even simple tasks, such as zipping up a jacket or operating a rescue flare. Persons immersed in cold water may be unable to assist in their own rescue.

Shivering tapers off and ceases as body temperature falls below 90° F (32° C), leading to a decrease in heat production. Violent shivering can lead to the metabolic production of acids, which accumulate in the blood, a condition known as acidosis. Shivering can also deplete the muscles of glycogen or glucose, which are necessary sources of energy for continued muscular activity—including shivering, although glycogen depletion takes many hours.

Brain

With mild core cooling, thinking processes and decision making become slower. Individuals become apathetic, irritable, and disagreeable. However, such persons should remain oriented and able to make correct decisions.

With more severe hypothermia, mental function is impaired to a far greater extent, leading to confusion, disorientation, and erroneous decision making. The desire or ability to obtain protection from the cold is progressively lost, leading to more rapid loss of body heat. Lethargy and somnolence progress in a waxing and waning manner to complete coma. During mild hypothermia slurred speech occurs as a function of the effect of cold on the muscles used for speech. At lower core temperatures, speech is impeded due to the effect of cold on the brain. Loss of vision occurs just prior to coma, a point at which a few hypothermic individuals take off their clothing (paradoxical disrobing) or climb out of sleeping bags.

Hypothermia markedly decreases the brain's need for oxygen. A normothermic person suffers irreversible damage if the brain is deprived of blood and the oxygen it carries for more than four or five minutes. When the brain is cold, it can tolerate a much longer time without oxygen before permanent damage occurs. This reduced oxygen need allows some individuals, particularly children, who have been submerged in cold water for as long as an hour, and some individuals who have been so severely hypothermic all heart function has ceased for that long or longer, to be successfully resuscitated without residual brain injury.

Circulatory System

The primary function of the circulatory system, which consists of the heart and the blood vessels, is to transport blood, which carries oxygen to the tissues and carbon dioxide away from them. One of the more devastating effects of severe hypothermia is a reduction in the volume of circulating blood. This reduction can be large enough to decrease blood flow and oxygen transport to a level below that needed for normal function. Vital organs such as the brain and heart, when not adequately perfused with oxygenated blood, cannot perform properly, which compounds the hypothermic situation.

Because their water losses exceed their water intake, essentially all hypothermic persons are dehydrated and have a reduced blood volume. Most hypothermic individuals are unable to obtain fluids, whether they are lying in a snowbank, immersed in cold water, or immobilized by Alzheimer's in a cold apartment. The longer the cold exposure lasts, the longer the period of inadequate fluid intake.

Hypothermia also increases fluid loss by producing cold diuresis—increased excretion of water by the kidneys. Cold diuresis is a complex phenomenon. Lying in one position for a long time increases urine flow. If a person is submerged in water, the hydrostatic pressure of the water on the skin squeezes fluid from the limbs (especially the legs) back into the body core. Intense constriction of blood vessels in the arms and legs, an attempt by the body to reduce heat loss in response to cooling, also forces blood back into the core. The body interprets this increased central blood volume as an indication that the body has retained too much fluid and decreases the production of antidiuretic hormone. This hormone causes the kidneys to conserve water, so a decrease in this hormone increases water loss through the kidneys. Finally, cold and insufficient oxygen directly affect the kidneys, decreasing their ability to conserve water and producing a larger urinary output.

The circulating blood volume is further decreased when the body is cooled because water leaves the circulating blood and is sequestered in the tissues. The viscosity of the blood can be greatly increased by the loss of fluid (hemoconcentration) and the direct effect of cold on the blood. Finally, cold induces contraction of the spleen, which increases the number of circulating red blood cells and thereby the blood viscosity. Thick, viscid blood imposes a greater work load on the heart.

HEART

At normal body temperatures the heart can force viscous blood through smaller vessels by pumping harder and faster. Unfortunately, when cooled to the level of severe hypothermia the heart pumps weakly and slowly. At such temperatures the heart muscle becomes stiff and weak, and the volume of blood pumped with each beat (the stroke volume) is markedly decreased.

As the body cools to such levels, the rate of impulse conduction through the nerves and special conductive tissue that control the heart becomes slower, and the number of beats per minute falls. With severe hypothermia the heart rate often falls below twenty beats per minute. Conduction also becomes erratic, contributing to irregularities of the heart beat, such as extra beats (extrasystoles) or atrial fibrillation, which reduce cardiac output (the volume of blood pumped by the heart), or ventricular fibrillation, which stops cardiac output entirely.

The muscle fibers of the heart must contract simultaneously in a well-coordinated sequence to pump blood. Fibrillation is a condition in which the individual muscle fibers contract rapidly in a totally unsynchronized, uncoordinated manner. Atrial fibrillation results in irregular conduction of the impulse to contract to the ventricle. Ventricular fibrillation renders the heart unable to pump blood. Such an event, untreated, is lethal within two or three minutes in normothermic individuals, although external cardiac compression (CPR) can keep some blood circulating for a longer time. The only treatment for ventricular fibrillation currently available is to electrically shock the heart and temporarily stop all of the fibers from contracting, with the hope that when they begin contracting again they will contract in a coordinated manner. Sometimes it works, although very rarely if the person's temperature is below 90° F (32° C).

A hypothermic heart is particularly susceptible to ventricular fibrillation. Minor irritants fully tolerated by the heart at normal temperatures (such as acidosis, hypocarbia, hypoxia, or even mechanical stimulation of the body) can cause a hypothermic heart to fibrillate. Once a cold heart fibrillates, restoring a normal rhythm with electrical shock is usually impossible.

When a person younger than twenty dies of hypothermia, the heart usually just slows down until its stops. Older individuals more often develop ventricular fibrillation.

A slow, weak heart pumping a reduced volume of thick, viscous blood that releases oxygen less readily, through narrowed blood vessels, cannot provide the tissues with an adequate oxygen supply. Without adequate oxygen, metabolism is incomplete. The products of incomplete metabolism are acids, mostly lactic and pyruvic acid. The accumulation of these acids in the tissues and in the blood causes acidosis (a lower pH), which also causes the heart to contract more weakly and erratically.

As the result of decreased fluid intake, increased fluid losses, and redistribution of the fluid that remains, victims of several days' exposure to cold sometimes have circulating blood volumes that have been reduced as much as 25 percent. An adequate water intake during cold exposure is absolutely essential.

Two additional changes decrease the transport of oxygen to the tissues. First, cold causes the blood vessels to constrict, reducing their diameter and increasing the resistance to flow. Second, most of the oxygen carried in the blood is bound to hemoglobin within the red blood cells. At the tissues hemoglobin normally releases oxygen, but cold hemoglobin releases its oxygen less readily. As a result, less oxygen is actually delivered to the tissues (Figure 2-1).

This diminished oxygen delivery is partially offset by two changes. First, the quantity of oxygen dissolved in the aqueous part of the blood (not carried by the hemoglobin in red blood cells) increases as it cools. At 86° F (30° C) the quantity of dissolved oxygen is 19 percent greater than at normal body temperature. Second, acidosis increases the rate of oxygen release by hemoglobin.

With all of these "disasters" occurring within the cardiovascular system, a severely hypothermic individual's blood pressure could certainly be expected to be low. Surprisingly, it is usually normal or nearly normal, although occasional individuals do have a low blood pressure. The blood pressure probably remains at normal levels because intense constriction of peripheral blood vessels, which increases the resistance to blood flow, maintains the pressure. The blood pressure may be very hard to measure with a standard cuff and stethoscope because the diminished blood flow

Figure 2-1. Oxyhemoglobin dissociation curve, the tendency for oxygen to leave hemoglobin and diffuse into tissues at different oxygen levels. As blood temperature decreases the curve shifts left, resulting in less off-loading of oxygen in the tissues.

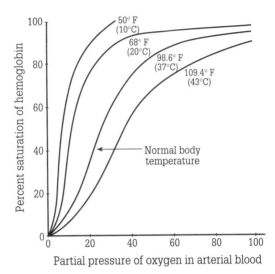

decreases the Korotkoff sounds by which pressure is measured. Automated sphygmomanometers, which do not depend on detecting Korotkoff sounds, may be more effective.

Lungs

The effects of hypothermia on the function of the lungs have not been as well studied as the effects on the heart and circulation. Ventilation, the movement of air into and out of the lungs, is known to be adequate until core temperature drops to about 86° to 90° F (30° to 32° C). At that temperature and below, carbon dioxide accumulates in the blood, indicating that ventilation is inadequate. Acidosis resulting from the accumulation of acidic metabolites is normally counterbalanced by increased ventilation. With severe hypothermia such respiratory compensation does not occur.

At normal body temperatures, the slight rise in carbon dioxide between breaths stimulates the brain to make the lungs take another breath and get rid of the carbon dioxide. With profound hypothermia, the brain—more specifically, the medullary respiratory centers—becomes unresponsive to carbon dioxide accumulation. The drive to breathe then derives from other sensors that are stimulated by low oxygen concentrations (hypoxia). Theoretically at least, treating hypothermia victims with oxygen could raise the blood concentration of oxygen to such levels that the hypoxic respiratory center would no longer be stimulated and the drive to breathe would be significantly reduced. Although an individual might not be hypoxic, more carbon dioxide would accumulate, which would further increase acidosis. Hypothermic individuals must not be over-ventilated. Hyperventilation lowers the blood carbon dioxide levels below normal, creating a condition called hypocarbia, which should be avoided because it makes a cold heart more susceptible to ventricular fibrillation.

Hypothermia may increase mucus secretion by the membranes lining the trachea and bronchi, the major air passages. The cough reflex may also be decreased, allowing the excessive mucus to collect within the passages. Additionally, stomach contents may be vomited and aspirated. Either of these events often leads to infection, which is sometimes severe. During rewarming, the lungs may fill with fluid (pulmonary edema). Autopsies of hypothermia victims often disclose lung abnormalities, which include infection (pneumonia), breakdown of the small air sacs (alveoli), bleeding, and fluid accumulation (edema).

OTHER CONSIDERATIONS

Cooling the liver, as with other organs, slows its metabolic functions, but such slowing has not caused any significant problems except with drug metabolism, much of which takes place in the liver. Any medication given to a hypothermic individual is metabolized more slowly, and its effects may last much longer. Giving drugs at intervals intended for normothermic individuals may lead to an overdose once the patient warms up. For this reason, drugs must be given cautiously or not at all during the treatment of hypothermia.

Acute pancreatitis, a serious medical complication in which the pancreas becomes inflamed and is often partially destroyed, occurs occasionally after severe hypothermia. Additionally, the effectiveness of insulin is blunted, perhaps as the result of inadequate release by the pancreas combined with reduced activity in the tissues due to the lower temperature. Increased blood sugar concentrations are not uncommon in hypothermic individuals, including those who are not diabetic.

Coagulopathies should be anticipated in hypothermia because clotting components do not function normally at low temperatures. Prothrombin time (PT) and partial thromboplastin time (PTT), two common measurements of clotting capability, are both prolonged by hypothermia alone.

The adrenal and thyroid glands seem to function well when cold, as evidenced by adequate concentrations of their hormones in the blood. The stomach may be affected by the stress, leading to ulcers, which occasionally cause significant bleeding. No typical changes occur in the blood sodium, potassium, or chloride concentrations.

COMPLICATIONS

In spite of the many pathologic changes occurring with hypothermia, hypothermia alone causes no permanent problems. All of the changes are completely reversible. No evidence indicates that individuals who have developed hypothermia are subsequently more susceptible to hypothermia or less tolerant of cold.

The complications that most commonly occur after rewarming are listed in the table below. However, for previously healthy persons, the risk of serious complications is low. Many of the complications result from preexisting, predisposing conditions, such as chronic alcoholism, malnutrition, or chronic debilitating diseases.

COMPLICATIONS OF SEVERE HYPOTHERMIA

Pneumonia
Acute pancreatitis
Intravascular clots (thromboses that cause myocardial infarcts and strokes)
Pulmonary edema
Acute renal failure
Increased renal potassium excretion leading to alkalosis
Hemolysis (breakdown of red blood cells)
Depressed bone marrow function
Inadequate blood clotting or disseminated intravascular coagulation
Low serum phosphorus
Seizures
Hematuria (blood in the urine)
Myoglobinuria (muscle pigment resembling hemoglobin in the urine)
Simian deformity of the hand
Temporary adrenal insufficiency
Gastric erosion or ulceration and bleeding

CHAPTER 3

Don't Lose Your Cool:
Mechanisms of Heat Loss

HEAT IS LOST FROM THE SKIN in four ways: convection, conduction, evaporation, and radiation. In the temperate surroundings in which most people live and work, 50 to 65 percent of the heat of metabolism is lost by radiation. Most of the remainder is lost through evaporation. Most clothing made of currently available materials does not effectively reduce these forms of heat loss.

In contrast, in a cold environment, convection is often the major source of heat loss, particularly if the air is moving. Heat loss by convection can be enormous in a strong wind. Conduction is a major route of heat loss during cold water immersion. Fortunately, heat loss by convection and conduction can be effectively reduced with available clothing materials.

RADIATION

Radiation, usually by far the largest source of heat loss, consists of the direct emission or absorption of heat energy. The human body continuously radiates heat to nearby solid objects that have a cooler temperature. Little heat is lost by radiation to the immediately surrounding air because it is a poor heat absorber, but all solid objects radiate heat to the atmosphere when they are not absorbing heat from the sun. Most of this radiant heat is in the form of infrared radiation; it is this radiation that allows warm bodies to be detected by infrared sensing devices.

In a calm, temperate climate of about 70° F (21° C) clothed, sedentary persons lose approximately 60 percent of their body heat through radiation. In a thermoneutral environment in which heat production equals heat loss by a nude human body, approximately 45 percent of heat loss is in the form of radiation.

Radiant heat loss is not well understood by many. An example of such loss occurs in small churches with stone walls that are only heated on the weekends in preparation for Sunday church services. Although the air in the church has been heated to 70° F (21° C), members of the congregation frequently feel cold and put on coats. The thick stone walls are still cold, and church occupants radiate heat to them, making them feel cold in spite of an air temperature that would be expected to be comfortable. The body also can gain large amounts of heat through radiation. The heat from the sun or a fire is radiant energy. This effect is seen during spring skiing. At a temperature normally uncomfortably cold, such as 32° F (0° C), skiers are able to ski in shirt sleeves because they are warmed by radiant heat from the bright sun.

In a cold climate nearby solid objects are colder and radiant heat loss is larger. The rate of heat loss increases dramatically as the difference in temperature between the body and the object increases—in fact, as the fourth powers of the two temperatures. The formula for measuring such heat loss is:

$$J_Q = -ek(T_s^4 - T_a^4)$$

J_Q = heat loss
e = the emissivity of the surface
k = the Stefan-Boltzmann constant
T_s = skin temperature (Kelvin or absolute)
T_a = ambient or atmospheric temperature (Kelvin or absolute)

The first item in the formula is the nature of the emitting surface, which emphasizes its significance: black or dark surfaces are better emitters than white or light-colored surfaces. However, radiation emitted by mammals is maximal regardless of skin pigmentation or the color of clothing.

Currently available clothing is of little benefit in reducing radiant heat loss because heat radiates from the body to the clothing and then radiates outward from the surface of the clothing. Attempts to cover clothing materials with a coating that would reflect heat back to the body have achieved little success. Microfilaments are claimed to reduce radiant heat loss, but the reductions are small and are lost with laundering. Light-colored clothing reduces radiant heat loss, but only to a very limited extent.

A layer of metallic (aluminum) foil on the outside of sleeping bags did significantly reduce radiative heat loss in recent studies. Such a layer was not effective for clothing, apparently because movement compresses the insulating layer.

Radiant heat loss becomes a major problem only in extremely cold situations—below -20° to -30° F (-29° to -35° C). If clothing adequately limits heat loss by other routes, particularly convection, physiologic mechanisms can compensate for the increased radiant heat loss encountered in most cold environments.

CONVECTION

Convective heat loss occurs whenever air—or water—that has a temperature below that of the body, contacts the skin, is warmed, and subsequently moves away. The heat that warmed the air is lost as the air moves away and the cooler air that replaces it also must be warmed.

An example of convection is the way soup is cooled by blowing on it. The soup warms the air just above its surface. Blowing moves this warm air away and replaces it with cool air that extracts more heat from the soup. Fans have been used since ancient times to take advantage of the cooling effect of moving air.

Convective heat loss is an essentially continuous process. Even though no wind is blowing, air warmed by the body expands, becomes lighter, rises, and is replaced by cooler air. In a thermoneutral environment approximately 40 percent of heat loss is convective.

Because convective heat loss can increase so enormously, it is the major cause of terrestrial hypothermia in the wilderness. Fortunately, clothing can greatly reduce this type of heat loss. Insulating clothing forms small pockets in which air is trapped—the essence of thermal insulation—and windproof outer garments prevent displacement of the air within and between layers. (Wet clothing loses its insulating ability, leading to greatly increased convective cooling.)

The amount of heat lost by convection is determined by the temperature difference between the air (water is discussed below) and the body surface with which it is in contact, and by the speed at which the air is moving. The greater the temperature difference the larger is the heat loss. However, little heat is required to increase the temperature of air (its specific heat—the amount of heat required to warm the air—is low), and low temperatures are well tolerated in still air.

Of far greater significance is the ability of moving air to remove large quantities of heat. In a wind the amount of heat lost increases as the square of the velocity—not in proportion to the velocity. A wind of 8 miles per hour (12.8 km/h) removes four times as much heat—not twice as much—as a wind of 4 miles per hour (6.4 km/h). At wind speeds above 40 miles per hour (64 km/h) heat loss increases only slightly because the air does not stay in contact with the body long enough to be warmed to skin temperature.

Wind chill is a term coined for the additional cooling produced by wind in a cold environment. Wind chill charts were originally derived from work published in 1945 by Paul Siple, who carried out many physiologic studies during Admiral Byrd's Antarctic expeditions. Siple compared the time it took water to freeze at different temperatures and wind conditions. Those conditions with similar freezing times were considered equivalent. However, unlike simple containers of water, humans produce heat metabolically and conserve heat through body fat and clothing. Therefore, water freezes faster than exposed human flesh. The older wind chill calculations overestimate the effect of wind chill and underestimate the freezing time. A new wind chill chart developed in 2001 was based on human exposure experiments, and was universally adopted (Figure A in color insert). Figure 3-1 illustrates how the old wind chill calculations predicted lower equivalent temperatures compared to the new calculations; the overestimation is shown at an air temperature of 5° F (-15° C) but the effect is similar at all air temperatures.

The effect of wind chill is illustrated by the following. In calm conditions, 20° F (-7° C) is somewhat warm for skiing, but a 10-mile-per-hour (16 km/h) wind produces cooling equivalent to a temperature of 9° F (-13° C), which is near the threshold that many skiers would tolerate. With a 20-mile-per-hour (32 km/h) wind, the equivalent temperature is 4° F (-16° C), and a 30-mile-per-hour wind produces cooling equivalent to -1° F (-18° C), which would drive all but the most ardent skiers into the lodges. (See Figure A in color insert for a contemporary wind chill chart in Fahrenheit and Celcius temperatures.)

The equations for calculating wind chill equivalent in Celsius and Fahrenheit temperatures are:

$$\text{WCE (°C)} = 13.12 + 0.6215T - 11.37(V_{0.16}) + 0.3965T(V_{0.16})$$
$$\text{WCE (°F)} = 35.74 + 0.6215T - 35.75(V_{0.16}) + 0.4275T(V_{0.16})$$

WCE = wind chill equivalent
T = air temperature
V = observed wind speed

Convective cooling is much greater in water than in air because the specific heat of water (the amount of heat required to warm the water) is

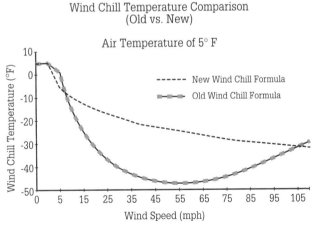

Figure 3-1. Comparison of old and new calculations of equivalent temperatures for various wind speeds at 5° F (-15° C)

far greater. Indeed, persons who are minimally insulated and fall into cold water lose heat less rapidly if they hold still because the convective cooling produced when the water is stirred by swimming is much greater than the heat generated by the physical activity.

CONDUCTION

Conduction is the direct transfer of heat away from the body by substances with which it is in direct contact. Air conducts heat poorly and calm air is an excellent insulator. Water has a conductivity approximately twenty-five times greater than air and is a good heat conductor. More importantly, water has about 3,500 times the volumetric heat capacity of air. (To raise the temperature of a specific volume of water a specific amount requires 3,500 times as much heat as would be required to raise the temperature of an identical volume of air the same amount.) Large amounts of heat are lost when the body is in contact with cold water even if movement and convective heat loss are minimized.

Stones and ice are good conductors and significant amounts of heat can be lost when sitting on them. Metal is an excellent heat conductor. Cold metal can produce almost instant freezing of tissues which it contacts, as many who have lost skin to cold mail boxes, garbage can lids, or ice trays can attest. The ground is a good conductor, and insulation such as foam pads is required by those sleeping on the ground to minimize heat loss. Air mattresses, which allow air to circulate freely, provide less insulation than foam pads. Heat can be lost through the soles of boots in contact with snow or ice if they are thin and not well insulated.

Although conductive heat loss alone is rarely a major cause of hypothermia, heat loss by this route can aggravate convective heat losses and should be avoided.

Alcohol (ethanol) is a good conductor that remains liquid at temperatures well below the freezing temperature of water. Reportedly a few intemperate residents of arctic climates have learned just how cold a beverage with high alcohol content can become when they have taken a swallow from a bottle left outside or in an unheated car during winter. The extremely cold alcohol almost instantly freezes the lips, tongue, and other tissues it contacts. If the liquid reaches the back of the throat and the esophagus, the resulting injury is often lethal.

The body gains heat by conduction when in contact with hot-water bottles or heating pads, or when immersed in a hot bath or a hot tub.

EVAPORATION

Evaporation is responsible for 20 to 30 percent of heat loss in temperate conditions. Through normal evaporative processes a sedentary person in a temperate climate loses approximately 300 kilocalories (kcal) daily, about 15 percent of his average daily food calorie intake.

Changing one gram of water on the skin from a liquid to a gas extracts approximately 0.58 kcal of heat, which is the reason perspiring is such an effective means of cooling.

About two-thirds of the evaporative heat loss in thermoneutral conditions occurs on the skin. In such situations the individual is not aware that he is sweating, but the skin is continually being moistened by insensible perspiration. Insensible perspiration continues in cold environments.

The remaining evaporative heat loss takes place in the air passages leading to the lungs. This also is an insensible water—and heat—loss. When air is inhaled, enough water is added by evaporation from the lining (mucosa) of the nose, throat, and trachea to bring the relative humidity of the inspired air to 100 percent, or saturation. In temperate climates the combined insensible water loss from the skin and respiratory tract is about 30 grams of water per hour, resulting in a heat loss of about 17 kilocalories per hour.

Heat loss through evaporation is obviously greatly increased by the heavy sweating associated with the high heat production of vigorous exercise or a hot environment. Surprisingly, evaporative heat losses may increase in a cold environment also.

Cold air is dry. Although the relative humidity of very cold air may be high, its actual water content is quite low. As the air is warmed to body temperatutre the relative humidity can drop to 1 or 2 percent. Therefore, more water is required to saturate the inspired air. In a cold climate more heat may be lost by evaporation to humidify inhaled air than is lost by warming the air to body temperature.

At high altitudes respirations are deeper and more rapid to compensate for the "thin" air. Several liters of water are required each day to humidify inhaled air. The evaporation of that amount of water extracts as much as 1,000 kilocalories and also can lead to dehydration, which aggravates the effects of hypothermia.

Evaporation of water from wet clothing causes great heat loss, particularly in a wind. Wet clothing is also a threat because it loses its insulating ability, leading to greatly increased convective cooling.

Mouth breathing increases fluid and heat loss somewhat, but the amount is insignificant in comparison with the quantity of heat lost through other sources. Winter outdoor enthusiasts, particularly high-altitude climbers, must be aware that this heat and water loss is occurring, must eat enough food to regenerate the heat, and must drink enough liquids to replace the water.

Airway cooling, however, can have a significant effect on sufferers of cold-induced asthma. For these people, wearing a moisture/heat exchange mask, or even a scarf over the mouth, can reduce airway cooling and respiratory heat and water loss.

Heat loss from the skin through insensible perspiration also cannot be effectively limited. Vapor-barrier systems, which consist of a layer of material that is impermeable to water vapor (usually plastic) between layers of insulation, have been tried. Theoretically, because the barrier prevents water vapor loss, perspiration would not evaporate, and heat loss by that route should be eliminated. However, perspiration does not cease, and the clothing underneath the barrier becomes saturated with water. Wet clothing has a decreased insulation value and no longer limits convective heat loss.

No vapor-barrier system works well at temperatures above freezing because too much water accumulates. Even at lower temperatures vapor-barrier systems have not been successful; the only one widely used has been in military footwear (Korean or "Mickey Mouse" boots) that is no longer being manufactured. Although such boots do keep feet warm, even frequent sock changes do not keep feet dry and antiperspirant must be applied to avoid injury by perpetual wetness.

CHAPTER 4

Too Cool to Breathe: Evaluation and Treatment of Hypothermia

HYPOTHERMIA IS PRODUCED by either excessive cold stress in active healthy adults or continued cooling in infants, the elderly, or those affected by a disease that has blunted or eliminated thermal defense mechanisms.

RISK FACTORS FOR HYPOTHERMIA

Increased Heat Loss
Cold exposure (wet/wind, immersion)
Cold infusions
Pharmacological agents/toxins
Burns/dermatitis

Decreased Heat Production
Infants/elderly
Malnutrition/hypoglycemia
Endocrinologic failure
Fatigue/exhaustion/trauma

Impaired Thermoregulation
Neuropathies/spinal injury
Diabetes mellitus
CNS failure
Trauma
Shock

HYPOTHERMIA RESULTS FROM INADEQUACIES
In wilderness environments, hypothermia results from:
- *Inadequate* protection from the cold
- *Inadequate* food for metabolic fuel to be burned during exercise
- *Inadequate* fluid intake resulting in dehydration

In urban environments, where hypothermia is significantly more common, the causes are:

○ *Inadequate* youth (old age) or maturity (infants and young children)
○ *Inadequate* money for housing, heat, clothing, and food
○ *Inadequate* sobriety

In both situations, inadequate "smarts" is an almost universal component of the cascade of events that leads to hypothermia.

DIAGNOSIS

Hypothermia can be divided into mild, moderate, and severe stages. These stages are defined by the *State of Alaska Cold Injuries Guidelines* and the *Practice Guidelines for Wilderness Emergency Care* by the Wilderness Medical Society, which also provide recommendations for basic to advanced treatment of hypothermia. Table 4-1 on page 41 lists the signs and symptoms used in the classification of the three levels of hypothermia.

Mild Hypothermia

The first response to cold stress includes a sensation of cold and shivering. Shivering is generally initiated before core temperature decreases and acts as a defensive measure to prevent or attenuate core cooling. Although these symptoms indicate a deficit in body heat balance, they are not necessarily indications that core temperature has fallen.

With mild hypothermia (core temperature of 95° to 90° F [35° to 32° C]), the thermoregulatory system functions normally. Shivering increases in intensity as core temperature drops, unless energy supply is limited (a process that takes several hours) or shivering is inhibited by drugs, alcohol, or physical trauma. Physical disability first impairs fine motor movements, but that is followed by gross motor failure. Mental impairment develops as core temperature approaches 90° F (32° C). Individuals experience loss of coordination and judgment and approach the limits of self-help. They have significant problems climbing into a life raft, climbing a ladder, lighting a flare, or performing other manual tasks.

At rest, a cold-exposed individual shivers. However, during exercise shivering may abate due to the heat production from exercise, making it difficult to diagnose the onset of hypothermia. Signs of a definite reduction in core temperature include slowing of pace, greater fatigue than other members of the group, muscular incoordination that leads to stumbling or falling, and intellectual and personality changes, particularly uncharacteristic irritability.

When core temperature falls to about 93° F (34° C), uncontrollable shivering develops and is quite easy to recognize. An individual should be considered to have mild hypothermia if he is cold but alert, vigorously shivering, and has normal vital signs.

A mnemonic useful for remembering the early stages of hypothermia is "umbles." The mildly hypothermic individual:

o Fumbles
o Stumbles
o Tumbles
o Mumbles
o Grumbles

The first three items reflect impairment of motor function, first fine movements and then gross movements. The last two indicate intellectual impairment.

Moderate and Severe Hypothermia

Moderate hypothermia is characterized by a core temperature ranging from 90° to 82° F (32° to 28° C). In this stage, thermoregulatory responses wane or disappear, and shivering decreases in intensity and eventually stops. Consciousness is usually lost at about 86° F (30° C), and cardiac dysrhythmias develop. People vary widely in their response to low core temperatures, however. Some individuals remain surprisingly alert. One person who had a measured rectal temperature of 86° F (30° C) was not only conscious but had driven his car a number of miles on an interstate freeway to get to a hospital emergency room.

Severe hypothermia is defined as a core temperature below 82° F (28° C), at which stage death is imminent. Acid-base abnormalities develop, and without rewarming the cold heart eventually goes into ventricular fibrillation followed by full cardiac arrest. Cardiac standstill can occur spontaneously at heart temperatures approaching 77° F (25° C) or can be induced by rough handling, and other mechanical stimulation, at core temperatures as high as 82° F (28° C).

A person with moderate to severe hypothermia could have the following signs and symptoms:

o Depressed vital signs, such as a slow pulse and slow respirations
o Staggering gait
o Altered level of consciousness, with slurred speech or lack of response to verbal or painful stimuli
o No shivering in spite of being very cold (a sign that may be altered by alcohol intoxication)

Moderate and severe hypothermia are usually easy to diagnose, but may be difficult to treat. As core temperature continues to fall and intellectual function deteriorates, individuals become confused or disoriented and often behave in odd ways. Typically, they do not protect themselves from the cold. They do not put on hats or mitts, coats are not zipped, and extra clothing is left in backpacks. Urinating in clothing is common. Muscular control also fails, as individuals progress from simply stumbling or falling, to being unable to walk without assistance. Eventually they cannot stand upright, and collapse.

Paradoxical undressing is a bizarre event in which very cold individuals loosen or remove some, or all, of their clothing. Some survivors have recounted an overwhelming feeling of warmth before they lost consciousness. Apparently, the blood vessels in the skin dilate at this stage, producing such a sensation of warmth that the person, in a cold-altered mental state, removes clothing or insulation. These actions result in more rapid core cooling, unconsciousness and, unless rescue occurs soon, death.

Moderate to severely hypothermic individuals must be handled as gently as possible. During these stages of hypothermia, metabolism is minimal and cardiorespiratory activity may be difficult to document. Persons in full cardiac arrest can survive for extended periods due to the protective effect of brain cooling. Unless obvious signs of a fatal injury are present, hypothermic individuals should not be declared dead until they have been rewarmed to a core temperature of at least 90° F (32° C) and further resuscitation efforts fail.

Core temperature measurements are, at best, difficult to make in the field and may be unnecessary. Both diagnosis and treatment of hypothermia can be based on the functional characteristics described above and listed in Table 4–1. A careful history can help determine whether hypothermia is primary (excessive heat loss) or secondary (the result of disease or age) or if symptoms are caused by other disorders such as trauma, drugs or alcohol, or diseases such as diabetes mellitus.

Table 4-1.
Classifications of Level of Hypothermia

Classifications	Core temp	Patient's ability to rewarm without external heat source	Clinical Presentation	
Normal	**Above 95¡F (35¡ C)**		**Cold sensation shivering**	
Mild	95–90° F (35–32° C)	Good	Physical impairment ▪Fine motor ▪Gross motor	Mental impairment ▪ Complex ▪ Simple
Moderate	90–82° F (32–28° C)	Limited	**Below 90¡F (32¡C) degrees shivering stops; below 86¡F (30¡C) consciousness is lost**	
Severe	Below 82 °F (28° C)	Unable	Rigidity Vital signs reduced or absent Severe risk of mechanically stimulated ventricular fibrillation (VF) (rough handling)	
	Below 77¡ F (25¡ C)	Unable	**Spontaneous ventricular fibrillation (VF) Cardiac arrest**	

Bold text shows the major thresholds between stages of hypothermia

RESCUE AND PREHOSPITAL TREATMENT
General Principles

Priority must be given to preventing anyone else from becoming a secondary victim during extraction of a hypothermic individual from a cold environment. Unless conditions, such as the threat of an avalanche, present an imminent hazard, a measured approach is preferable to fast, radical actions. Hypothermia, unlike choking or cardiac arrest, does not present a true medical emergency. Hypothermia develops over a period of time; terrestrial hypothermia occurs over several hours to days, while immersion hypothermia generally requires thirty minutes to a few hours. With either disorder, the person's condition does not worsen precipitously in the few extra minutes needed to effect a safe, gentle rescue. On the other hand, hurried, rough handling could trigger ventricular fibrillation, creating a true, usually fatal, medical emergency.

Individuals who are cold stressed but not yet hypothermic may be lightly shivering but behaving normally. Such persons can be warmed by exercise, for example, by walking or skiing to a shelter or by working to set up a campsite. On the other hand, if the individual actually seems hypothermic and is either suffering from the "umbles," shivering vigorously and uncontrollably, or exhibiting signs of more advanced hypothermia, he should be removed from the cold environment and placed in a prone position. Measures should be taken to prevent further heat loss, and the Emergency Medical Service (EMS) should be activated if possible.

Wet clothing increases surface heat loss considerably and should be removed once the individual is sheltered from extreme environmental conditions. A mildly hypothermic person may assist in removing wet clothing, but if the individual is moderately to severely hypothermic (shivering is waning or absent, and consciousness is altered) wet clothing should be cut off. In either case the individual should be packaged for treatment in the field or for transport to medical care (Figure 4-1).

Packaging should follow the general principles of the hypothermia wrap commonly used by search and rescue (SAR) groups. The wrap should be a single integrated system that includes as much insulation as practical, including ground pads and multiple sleeping or insulating bags, and a vapor barrier. The insulation decreases conductive and convective heat loss, and the vapor barrier decreases convective and evaporative heat loss. The vapor barrier would normally be wrapped around the outside of the insulation to prevent snow or rain from wetting the insulation. However, the vapor barrier could be placed inside the insulation if the person is wet and cannot be dried. If the elements of a hypothermia wrap are not available, or implementation is not practical, the individual should be moved to the best shelter available, and efforts made to remove as much water from clothing as possible.

The priorities for treatment are arresting the fall in core temperature, establishing a safe rewarming rate while maintaining the stability of

Figure 4-1. Hypothermia wrap for packaging a cold individual. Clothing should be removed and the person should be moved—once only—into the wrap, which includes insulating pads and covers, and a vapor barrier.

the cardiovascular system, and providing physiological support through oxygenation, correction of metabolic and electrolyte imbalances, and fluid replenishment, intravenously if possible. Individuals should be classified as mildly hypothermic or moderately to severely hypothermic by their level of shivering, physical impairment, and level of consciousness. Core temperature (preferably esophageal) can be used as an adjunct diagnostic tool if available, but is not essential.

Treatment for Mild Hypothermia

If no way to get to a medical facility is available or more than thirty minutes is required to arrive at a medical facility, a hypothermic person should be rewarmed by one or more of the following methods. Shivering is a very effective process for increasing heat production and a vigorously shivering individual should warm effectively when well insulated. Shivering should be fueled by calorie replacement with fluid containing sugars. (The sugar content is more important than the heat in warm drinks.) Individuals should not be allowed to drink liquids unless they are capable of swallowing without aspirating. Alcohol or tobacco use should not be permitted.

If an external heat source is available and practical, it should be applied to areas of high surface-heat transfer, particularly the underarm areas and sides of the chest. The head and neck are theoretically efficient for heat transfer, but may be impractical to heat. The groin should be avoided because it is farther from the heart than the underarm areas and is at greater risk for accidental burns. In a vigorously shivering person, active heating warms the skin, decreases shivering heat production, and results in a rewarming rate similar to shivering alone (Figure 4-2). However, active warming is not contraindicated; it is beneficial because it increases comfort, preserves energy stores, and reduces cardiovascular stress.

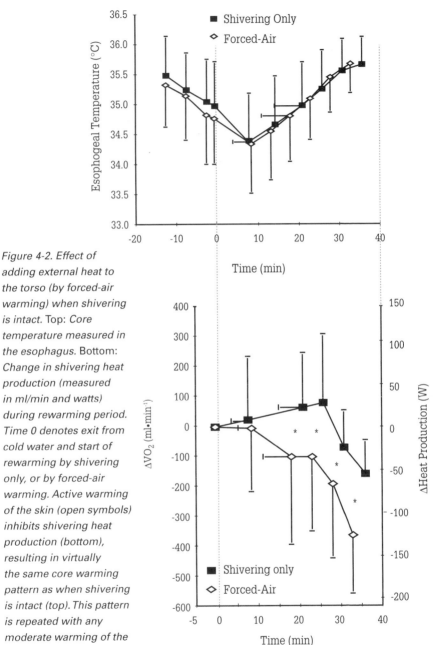

Figure 4-2. Effect of adding external heat to the torso (by forced-air warming) when shivering is intact. Top: *Core temperature measured in the esophagus.* Bottom: *Change in shivering heat production (measured in ml/min and watts) during rewarming period. Time 0 denotes exit from cold water and start of rewarming by shivering only, or by forced-air warming. Active warming of the skin (open symbols) inhibits shivering heat production (bottom), resulting in virtually the same core warming pattern as when shivering is intact (top). This pattern is repeated with any moderate warming of the skin, including body-to-body warming or electric or charcoal heaters.*

External sources of heat such as hot-water bottles or direct contact with a warm body may be provided by a hypothermic individual's companions. Search and rescue (SAR) personnel may carry devices such as charcoal heaters (Figure 4-3), and Emergency Medical Service (EMS) personnel may have facilities for forced-air warming (Figure 4-4). Hot-water bottles can burn the

Figure 4-3. Left: *Charcoal heater. Charcoal fuel (in metal canister) is ignited and placed in combustion chamber (center of photo). Heated air is blown through impermeable flexible tubing. Exhaust exits through black tube. An insulated cover is placed over the chamber to prevent burning the skin.* Right: *Charcoal heater in use. Combustion chamber is placed on the chest with flexible tubing applied to other areas of high heat transfer such as the neck and armpits. Initial ignition produces smoke but subsequent operation is safe in any ventilated area. One charcoal briquette supports heat production of 250 watts for eight to twelve hours.*

 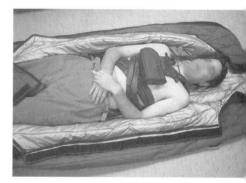

Figure 4-4. Left: *Forced-air warming system with Bair Hugger and folding rigid torso cover.* Right: *System in use in a United States Coast Guard rescue helicopter. It can be used in any transport vehicle equipped with an inverter that produces 120 VAC and 10 amps.*

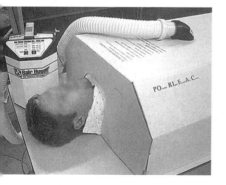 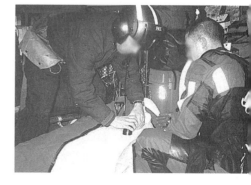

skin. They should be wrapped in a piece of clothing and held in a rescuer's armpit for a minute or so to insure they are not too hot. The charcoal heater is the most effective portable rewarming device. It contains a slowly burning charcoal fuel canister and a fan that circulates the heat through flexible tubing. It contributes 250 watts of heat directly to the skin for eight to twelve hours and requires only a single D-cell battery to power the fan.

Chemical heat packs are used regularly, but their effectiveness for treating hypothermia is marginal. Smaller packs—such as hand and foot warmers—have very limited heat capacity and do not appreciably warm a cold subject. They are useful, however, if placed on the hands and feet to prevent frostbite during treatment and transport. Larger chemical heat packs have more heat capacity, but they usually have an initial spike in temperature to 130°–150° F (54°–66° C), which poses a burn risk to the individual. This spike is followed quickly by a fall in temperature to ineffective levels. The pack must be insulated from the person, wasting valuable heat. Finally, heat packs have a finite heat capacity and do not guarantee a final surface temperature. If the packs are initially cold, they warm to lower temperatures and are even less effective.

Light exercise, such as walking, produces heat and may be helpful, but should be performed only after a mildly hypothermic individual is dry, has had calorie replacement, and has been stable for at least thirty minutes. Such individuals must be closely monitored until recovery to normothermia is complete.

A warm shower or bath may be tolerated by a mildly hypothermic individual who is alert and mobile. However, if signs of moderate to severe hypothermia are present, warm water immersion could cause sudden death and is contraindicated.

More sophisticated care may be possible if SAR or EMS personnel are involved. If oxygen is available, it should be heated to a maximum of 108° F (42° C) and humidified. Heated humidified oxygen does not significantly warm the body core but does assist rehydration and may warm the upper airway and the brain structures that include the cardiorespiratory and thermoregulatory control centers. Indications for intravenous (IV) fluids are the same for mildly hypothermic individuals as they are for normothermic persons (see below).

Persons with mild hypothermia can return to a cold environment if they are provided with additional clothing. They must not be sent out into the same conditions in which they became hypothermic without additional protection.

Treatment for Moderate to Severe Hypothermia with Signs of Life

For an individual with moderate to severe hypothermia, extraction must be as gentle as possible to avoid precipitating ventricular fibrillation. The extremities should not be rubbed or manipulated. The body should be horizontal to preserve cardiovascular stability. Once removed from imminent danger, wet clothing should be cut off, and the person should be transferred in one motion to a packaging system for transport to more advanced medical care (to an ambulance or helicopter and then to a hospital). Packaging should follow the general principles of the hypothermia wrap previously described.

For moderately to severely hypothermic persons, cardiac monitors should be applied, intravenous catheters should be inserted if available, and a neurologic exam should be conducted to rule out head and neck injury. A core temperature should be obtained if possible; an esophageal probe is preferable.

If individuals have signs of life—detectable respirations or a pulse—they should be rewarmed as outlined above with the following exceptions. The individuals must not be allowed to sit or stand until rewarmed. Under no circumstances should moderately to severely hypothermic individuals be placed in a warm shower or bath, which could cause cardiovascular and metabolic instability and sudden death. These individuals should not be given oral fluids or food, and no attempts should be made to increase heat production through exercise, including walking.

In any hypothermic individual, core temperature continues to decrease after removal from the cold stress, a phenomenon referred to as afterdrop. Afterdrop may be pronounced and may last for many hours in a moderately to severely hypothermic person who is not shivering and who may have a metabolic heat production that is less than 50 percent of normal—about 50 watts (Figure 4-5). Since the common terminal event in hypothermia is cardiac arrest or ventricular fibrillation, the risk for which is a function of low heart temperature and the time spent at that temperature, even gradual warming of the heart is beneficial.

Most mildly to severely hypothermic individuals are volume depleted and may require aggressive fluid administration. However, starting IV fluids in cold individuals is difficult because their peripheral blood vessels are constricted. Transport, communication with rescue services, or other therapy should not be delayed by prolonged efforts to start an IV. The recommended fluids for rehydration are normal saline or glucose (D5W). Bolus therapy is preferable to a continuous drip. The individual can be given a 250 cc bolus and the IV either saline locked, which is preferable, or the flow of fluids decreased to a rate that just keeps the IV open (which would not be practical in freezing environments). Additional boluses can be delivered as needed to correct the fluid deficit. IV fluids should be heated to 104° to 108° F (40° to 42° C) when possible, but at worst should be no colder than the person's core temperature. They can be warmed to some extent by placing them inside a rescuer's jacket.

The subject's status must be reassessed periodically, and the individual should be transferred to a medical facility as soon as possible.

Treatment for Severe Hypothermia with No Signs of Life

A person with severe hypothermia with no signs of life must be handled very carefully. An examination for pulse and respirations should last at least sixty seconds; heart rate and breathing frequency may be very slow and detection may be difficult in a cold, stiff body. If breathing and pulse are not detected, three minutes of ventilation should be given—mouth-to-mouth if necessary. Such oxygenation may improve cardiorespiratory activity enough for it to be detected.

After three minutes of ventilation, the individual should be reexamined for pulse and respiration for a further sixty seconds. If breathing and pulse are still undetected, continuing ventilations and chest compressions (cardiopulmonary resuscitation or CPR) may be considered (Figure 4-6).

A cardiac monitor should be applied, if one is available. A portable electrocardiograph (ECG or EKG) may not distinguish between fibrillation, absent heartbeat, and artifacts (particularly those introduced by shivering), but it

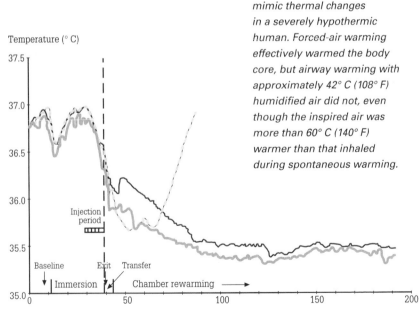

Figure 4-5. Continued decrease in core temperature (afterdrop) after a nonshivering human is removed from cold water immersion, insulated, and placed in -20° C (-4° F) air. The afterdrop is pronounced and extends for several hours. (Heavy line represents unwarmed controls, medium line individuals receiving heated, humidified airway rewarming, and circles individuals given forced air rewarming.) Shivering is inhibited by meperidine (Demerol) to mimic thermal changes in a severely hypothermic human. Forced-air warming effectively warmed the body core, but airway warming with approximately 42° C (108° F) humidified air did not, even though the inspired air was more than 60° C (140° F) warmer than that inhaled during spontaneous warming.

Time from cold water exit (minutes)

Fahrenheit	32	23	14	5	-4	-13	-22	-31	-40	-49	-58
Celsius	*0*	*-5*	*-10*	*-15*	*-20*	*-25*	*-30*	*-35*	*-40*	*-45*	*-50*
Wind Speed				Equivalent Temperatures							
3.1 mph	28	19	9	-2	-11	-22	-33	-42	-53	-63	-72
5 kph	*-2*	*-7*	*-13*	*-19*	*-24*	*-30*	*-36*	*-41*	*-47*	*-53*	*-58*
6.1 mph	27	16	5	-6	-17	-27	-38	-49	-60	-71	-81
10 kph	*-3*	*-9*	*-15*	*-21*	*-27*	*-33*	*-39*	*-45*	*-51*	*-57*	*-63*
9.2 mph	25	12	1	-9	-20	-31	-42	-54	-65	-76	-87
15 kph	*-4*	*-11*	*-17*	*-23*	*-29*	*-35*	*-41*	*-48*	*-54*	*-60*	*-66*
12.2 mph	23	10	0	-11	-22	-35	-45	-56	-69	-80	-90
20 kph	*-5*	*-12*	*-18*	*-24*	*-30*	*-37*	*-43*	*-49*	*-56*	*-62*	*-68*
15.3 mph	21	10	-2	-13	-26	-36	-47	-60	-71	-83	-94
25 kph	*-6*	*-12*	*-19*	*-25*	*-32*	*-38*	*-44*	*-51*	*-57*	*-64*	*-70*
18.3 mph	21	9	-4	-15	-27	-38	-51	-62	-74	-85	-98
30 kph	*-6*	*-13*	*-20*	*-26*	*-33*	*-39*	*-46*	*-52*	*-59*	*-65*	*-72*
21.4 mph	19	7	-4	-17	-27	-40	-53	-63	-76	-87	-99
35 kph	*-7*	*-14*	*-20*	*-27*	*-33*	*-40*	*-47*	*-53*	*-60*	*-66*	*-73*
24.4 mph	19	7	-6	-17	-29	-42	-54	-65	-78	-90	-101
40 kph	*-7*	*-14*	*-21*	*-27*	*-34*	*-41*	*-48*	*-54*	*-61*	*-68*	*-74*
27.5 mph	18	5	-6	-18	-31	-44	-54	-67	-80	-92	-103
45 kph	*-8*	*-15*	*-21*	*-28*	*-35*	*-42*	*-48*	*-55*	*-62*	*-69*	*-75*
30.5 mph	18	5	-8	-20	-31	-44	-56	-69	-81	-76	-105
50 kph	*-8*	*-15*	*-22*	*-29*	*-35*	*-42*	*-49*	*-56*	*-63*	*-60*	*-76*
33.6 mph	18	5	-8	-20	-33	-45	-58	-71	-81	-94	-107
55 kph	*-8*	*-15*	*-22*	*-29*	*-36*	*-43*	*-50*	*-57*	*-63*	*-70*	*-77*
36.6 mph	16	3	-9	-22	-33	-45	-58	-71	-83	-96	-108
60 kph	*-9*	*-16*	*-23*	*-30*	*-36*	*-43*	*-50*	*-57*	*-64*	*-71*	*-78*
39.7 mph	16	3	-9	-22	-35	-47	-60	-72	-85	-98	-110
65 kph	*-9*	*-16*	*-23*	*-30*	*-37*	*-44*	*-51*	*-58*	*-65*	*-72*	*-79*
42.7 mph	16	3	-9	-22	-35	-47	-60	-72	-85	-98	-112
70 kph	*-9*	*-16*	*-23*	*-30*	*-37*	*-44*	*-51*	*-58*	*-65*	*-72*	*-80*
45.8 mph	14	1	-11	-24	-36	-49	-62	-74	-87	-99	-112
75 kph	*-10*	*-17*	*-24*	*-31*	*-38*	*-45*	*-52*	*-59*	*-66*	*-73*	*-80*
48.8 mph	14	1	-11	-24	-36	-49	-62	-76	-89	-101	-114
80 kph	*-10*	*-17*	*-24*	*-31*	*-38*	*-45*	*-52*	*-60*	*-67*	*-74*	*-81*

Figure A. Wind chill equivalent temperatures using the new calculations. Green indicates low risk of frostbite; yellow indicate increasing risk within thirty minutes of exposure; orange indicates high risk within ten minutes of exposure; darker orange indicates high risk within five minutes of exposure; and the red zone indicates high risk within two minutes of exposure.

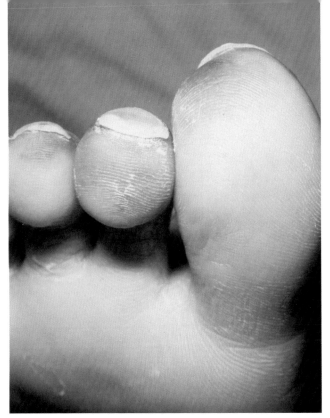

Figure B

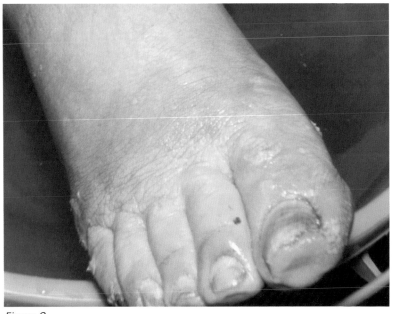

Figure C

Opposite: *Figure B. Violaceous discoloration of the tips of the first three toes indicating mild frostbite. (This injury occurred in a young climber who was unaware that he had frostbite until he took off his boots in camp. No tissue loss resulted.)* Photograph courtesy of Cameron C. Bangs, M.D.

Opposite: *Figure C. Very early, mild frostbite of the toes and distal foot (blanched area) during rapid rewarming. Eventual tissue loss was limited to toe nails.* Photograph courtesy of Bruce C. Paton, M.D.

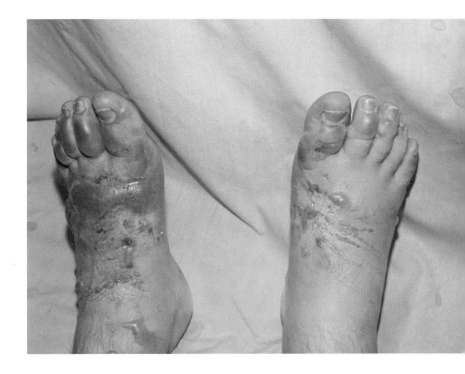

Figure D. Blisters filled with clear fluid and blisters filled with bloody fluid, neither extending to tips of toes, in relatively severe frostbite of the feet. (This injury resulted from sitting in the snow, meditating, with no protection for the feet but sneakers, for four hours.) Photograph courtesy of Bruce C. Paton, M.D.

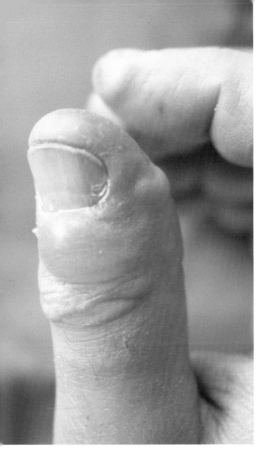

Figure E. (Left) *Bluish discoloration of the thumbnail and fingertips and a blister filled with clear fluid proximal to the nail (not extending to the tip of the thumb) in frostbite of moderate severity. (This injury occurred when a male climber took off one mitten only for long enough to urinate during a severe blizzard. The other hand was not injured. The photograph was taken one day later.)*

Figure F. (Below) *Blackened thumb tip and dark purple finger tips of the same hand one week later. (The site of the blister has a normal color and was less severely injured than the more distal tissues, which did not blister.)*

Photographs courtesy of Cameron C. Bangs, M.D.

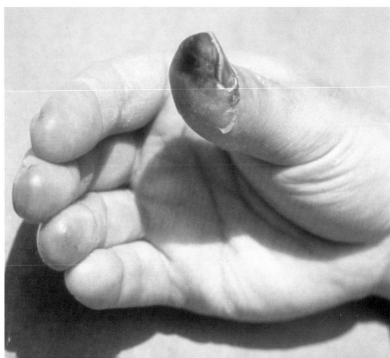

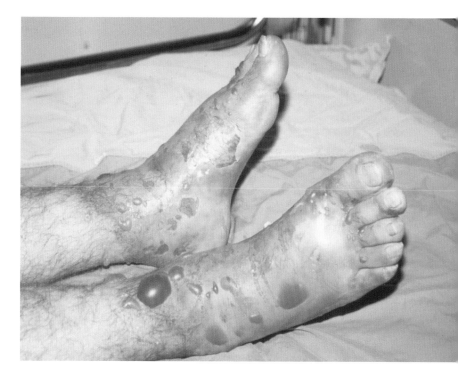

Figure G. Bluish discoloration, distal areas with no blisters, and more proximal areas covered by blisters, some filled with bloody fluid, on feet that have suffered severe frostbite. (This injury occurred in a man who spent twelve hours in a refrigerated railroad boxcar at 0° F (-18° C) wearing snugly laced, high top boots. His feet and ankles, which had their circulation impaired by the boots, were the only tissues that suffered cold injury. Seven weeks after injury, the tissues not covered by blisters in this photograph are those that died, illustrating the difficulty of predicting the severity of tissue loss. Tissues covered by blisters containing bloody fluid usually die. Photograph courtesy of Cameron C. Bangs, M.D.

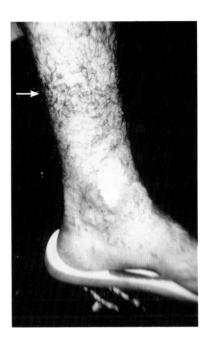

Figure H. Immersion foot. The arrow indicates the top of the boot.

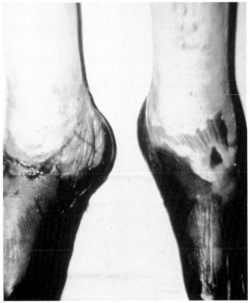

Figure I. Severe immersion foot in an Argentine soldier of the Falklands war who wore his boots constantly for forty-four days without taking them off.

Photograph courtesy of the Argentine Navy Medical Department

Figure J. (Above) *Rescuer using a throw bag to pull an immersed subject to shore. The victim has been instructed to wrap the rope around his arm because he may be unable to hold on to the rope if he is cold.*

Figure K. (Left) *Fully equipped rescuer with insulated dry suit and helmet, flotation sling, and flotation sled.*

Figure L. Three phases of vehicle submersion.

Top: *Floating—water level below the bottom of the side windows.*

Middle: *Sinking—water level above windows with water rising in the car but below the outside water level; pressure differences prevent the door from being opened.*

Bottom: *Submerged—water has filled the car, the doors can easily be opened but no air is available for individuals to breathe. The best strategy is to exit during the floating stage following the sequence: Seat belts off; Children unbuckled; Windows open; Out, children first, through windows as quickly as possible.*

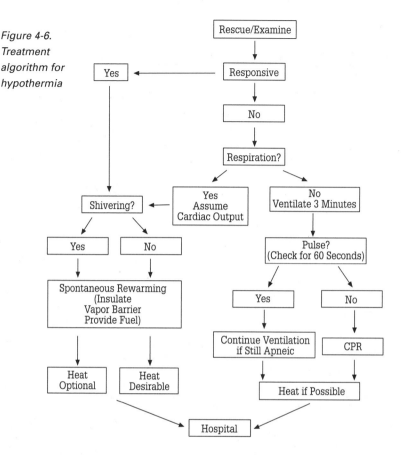

Figure 4-6.
Treatment
algorithm for
hypothermia

can identify QRS complexes indicative of a beating heart. If the individual is in ventricular fibrillation, one series of defibrillation attempts is reasonable. If successful the individual should be transported immediately to the nearest medical facility. If unsuccessful, and core temperature is below 86° F (30° C), no further attempts at defibrillation should be made, but the person should still be transported immediately to the nearest medical facility. As core temperature rises above 86° F (30° C), the likelihood of successful defibrillation increases, so for individuals with temperatures above that level, defibrillation attempts should be carried out as if they were normothermic.

If the cold heart is in asystole—as assessed in two different ECG leads—defibrillation should not be attempted. CPR should be considered and the individual transported to a medical facility. If the cardiac monitor shows any rhythm other than ventricular fibrillation or asystole, chest compressions should not be started because they would usually trigger ventricular fibrillation.

CPR for severely hypothermic individuals should be initiated only in a few narrowly defined situations.

- CPR must be performed only in situations that are safe for the rescuers. The probability of success is small and placing others at risk of an avalanche or similar hazard cannot be justified.
- CPR must not delay evacuation to a hospital. If the individual can be transported to a hospital, CPR should be started only after placement in the transport vehicle.
- CPR must not be initiated if the individual shows any signs of life. The subject must clearly not have any effective heart action. CPR for a severely hypothermic person with a heartbeat, regardless of how slow, usually induces ventricular fibrillation.
- CPR must not be contraindicated by other conditions, such as associated severe illness or obvious life-threatening injury, a noncompressible chest, ice formation in the airway, or witnessed prolonged cardiac inactivity.

A multicenter survey found that nine of twenty-seven individuals for whom CPR was started in the field survived, as did six of fourteen subjects for whom CPR was initiated in the emergency department. Successful resuscitation has been achieved after CPR as long as 220 and 390 minutes. Even intermittent CPR during litter evacuation has been successful. Therefore CPR probably should be started if the listed criteria can be met, and if enough rescue personnel are available to carry out prolonged CPR without becoming exhausted.

Once CPR is initiated in the field, deciding when to stop can be difficult, particularly if a supervising physician is not available. Jurisdictional and situational differences make it difficult to establish a standard protocol. For instance the State of Alaska allows EMTs, paramedics, physician assistants, and physicians to pronounce a person dead if thirty minutes of CPR, while attempting to rewarm the subject, are unsuccessful. Alternatively, continuing CPR for several hours does not appear unreasonable in view of the successes described above, assuming the individual can be rewarmed.

Mouth-to-mouth or mouth-to-mask breathing, or bag-and-valve ventilation with oxygen, should be carried out at half the normal rate (six breaths per minute) to prevent hyperventilation. Hypothermic individuals have greatly reduced oxygen demands and produce little carbon dioxide. Ventilation at a normal rate produces a low blood carbon dioxide level—hypocarbia—that predisposes a cold heart to ventricular fibrillation. In addition, hypothermic myocardium loses much of its compliance. Slower CPR allows more time for the heart to fill between compressions.

Unfortunately, there is no completely reliable indication that a hypothermic individual is irrecoverably dead. The adage "no one is dead until they are warm and dead" is widely accepted. Even apparent rigor mortis, dependent lividity, or dilated and fixed pupils are not indicators that CPR should be withheld. In several studies, individuals with a serum potassium concentration of more than 10 mmol/l have been unresuscitatable. Some centers use this serum potassium concentration, an arterial pH lower than 6.5, and a core temperature below 53.6° F (12° C) as criteria that cardiopulmonary bypass rewarming should not be started. However, those parameters can rarely be measured in a wilderness situation.

Treatment of Severe Hypothermia in Remote Areas

If shelter is available, the person should be moved into it—carried in a horizontal position to avoid pooling of blood in the legs. If the shelter is a tent, it should be pitched at a site that minimizes the distance the subject must be transported. Snow caves are warmer. A stove should not be used inside the shelter unless it is well ventilated; carbon monoxide accumulates in poorly ventilated enclosures.

Wet clothing should normally be cut off to avoid moving the subject. If no sleeping bags or other insulative covers are available, and no dry clothing for replacement is on hand, the person's wet clothing may have to be gently removed, wrung out, and gently replaced. Some fabrics, particularly wool, pile or fleece, and garments filled with man-made fibers such as polyesters, retain much of their insulating capabilities when wet. In contrast, wet cotton and saturated down-filled garments are almost worthless.

Hypothermic individuals should be insulated from the ground, snow, or whatever surface they are lying on. Insulated sleeping pads are ideal, but clothing, backpacks, other equipment, or even evergreen boughs may be used if necessary.

The person must be protected from the environment—low temperature, wind, and wetness—with dry clothing, sleeping bags (more than one if available), and a vapor barrier. Constricting clothing, particularly boots, should be loosened (but not removed) to reduce the risk of frostbite.

A fire should be built, if possible, with a reflective surface behind it to direct heat toward the individual being treated and caregivers. A fire does not effectively warm an insulated hypothermic person (radiative heat loss from body surfaces not facing the fire is still significant) but does help keep him dry and decreases further heat loss. It also provides warmth to the rescuers and facilitates drying wet clothing, sleeping bags, or other gear. Care must be taken to prevent the hypothermic individual from being burned by being placed too close to the fire.

If a severely hypothermic person can be insulated properly, external heat must be applied to the chest and underarms. In a remote area where the victim cannot be transported and must await SAR or EMS personnel, warming can be accomplished by methods described earlier. Any source of heat applied consistently over time provides some advantage over no warming at all.

Field rewarming may be a slow process; twenty-four hours or more may be required. Rescuers must have the equipment (tents, sleeping bags, and protective clothing) and the supplies (fuel, food, and water) they need to survive unharmed for that period of time. Severe weather, such as a snowstorm with high winds, is a threat to rescuers as well as hypothermic individuals. Evacuation to a medical facility as soon as safely possible should be a priority.

HOSPITAL TREATMENT
Monitoring Temperature

Within a hospital, temperature monitoring is best accomplished with an esophageal temperature probe inserted (gently) approximately 17 inches (42 cm) past the external nares. Rectal temperature measurements are less reliable because they lag behind heart and esophageal temperatures, both during cooling and after rewarming has started.

A tympanic membrane temperature probe would be reliable, but care must be taken to prevent perforation of the ear drum, and the ear must be adequately insulated to prevent thermal contamination of the ear canal. Infrared tympanic membrane temperature measurements have not been reliable in clinical practice. Temperature probes in Foley catheters are not reliable. Central intravascular temperature probes are reliable, but must remain outside the right atrium to avoid precipitating cardiac dysrhythmias. Pulmonary artery temperature probes carry the risk of producing dysrhythmias, and also can perforate the cold pulmonary artery.

General Measures

The most informative blood tests include a complete blood count, electrolytes, and glucose. Arterial blood gasses may also be obtained, but uncorrected values, not "temperature-corrected" values, should be used. Normal blood gas concentrations and pH levels at any other temperature are not the same as at 98.6° F (37° C). (The neutral pH of water is 7.0 at 25° C, but is 6.8 at 37° C.) Blood gas and pH determinations for hypothermic individuals must not be corrected for temperature because tables of normal values for lower (or higher) temperatures are almost never available. Blood samples are warmed to 98.6° F (37° C) in the laboratory before the determinations are made. Thus, evaluating the person's status by comparing uncorrected pH and blood gas levels with normal values at 98.6° F (37° C) is entirely appropriate, is much easier, and is far less likely to lead to erroneous therapy.

A chest x-ray and 12-lead electrocardiogram should be obtained. Endotracheal intubation and ventilation should be carried out unless protective airway reflexes are present. End-tidal CO_2 should be monitored. A nasogastric tube should be inserted if the individual is in moderate or severe hypothermia. An in-dwelling urinary bladder catheter should be used to monitor urine output.

Sedation should not be used to suppress shivering when hypothermia is the primary problem. Naloxone may reduce the severity of hypothermia with drug overdose or spinal shock.

If myxedemic coma is suspected, thyroid function studies should be obtained and serum cortisol levels should be measured.

Acid-base, fluid, and electrolyte imbalances should be corrected. A central venous pressure line can be inserted to monitor fluid status. Intravenous glucose, saline, or glucose in saline can be administered as a 250 cc bolus (20 cc/kg for children) and repeated as indicated. Most individuals who do not have contraindications, such as pulmonary edema, usually require at least one liter of fluids. IV fluids should be heated to 104–108° F (40–42° C) prior to administration.

Coagulopathies should be anticipated in hypothermia because clotting components do not function normally at low temperatures. Prothrombin time (PT) and partial thromboplastin time (PTT) are both prolonged by hypothermia. Heparinization is required for bypass if heparin-bonded tubing is not available. Disseminated intravascular coagulation (DIC) should be anticipated during and following this procedure.

Defibrillation can be initially attempted at 2 watt sec/kg up to 200 watt sec. Two further attempts may be made at 360 watt sec. If unsuccessful, the person should be warmed, while being treated with CPR or cardiopulmonary bypass, to a core temperature above 86° F (30° C) before further defibrillation attempts.

Medications are generally contraindicated because increased protein binding and decreased metabolism render the drugs ineffective during hypothermia and predispose the subject to overdose following warming. Pharmacological interventions should await warming to core temperatures above 86° F (30° C).

Hypothermia compromises host defenses and may result in serious bacterial infections, which can be accompanied by minimal inflammatory responses. Bone marrow release and circulation of neutrophils are compromised for up to twelve hours. Children and the elderly are more prone to sepsis. Prophylactic care includes administration of an aminoglycoside with a broad-spectrum β–lactam antibiotic. Antibiotic prophylaxis is not usually indicated for previously healthy adults, but should be considered following a failure to rewarm, or in the presence of any evidence of aspiration, myositis, chest radiographic infiltrates, bacteriuria, or a persistent altered mental status.

Rewarming Techniques

Rewarming methods can be classified according to:
- o   The amount of heat produced (low-to-moderate and nonaggressive; high and aggressive)

Table 4-2. Rewarming heat sources and effectiveness for hypothermia and frostbite.

Power Source	Heat Level/ Aggressive	Heat Source		Treatment Effectiveness	
		PRE-HOSPITAL	HOSPITAL	Hypothermia	Frostbite
Non-Electric	Low-to-Moderate Heat **Non-Aggressive**	Fire		XX	XXX
		Chemical Pack		–	✓
		IV Fluid		✓	–
		Warm Sweet Drink		✓	–
		Inhalation Warming		–	–
		Warm Water Bottles		✓	✓
		Warm Body		✓	✓
		Charcoal Heat Pack		✓✓	✓
Electric 120 VAC		Electric Blanket	Electric Blanket	✓	✓
		Water Blanket	Water Blanket	✓	✓
		Forced-Air Warming	Forced-Air Warming	✓✓	✓
	High Heat **Aggressive**	Warm Shower		XX	–
		Warm Bath	Warm Bath	XXX	–
			Lavage	✓✓✓	–
			CAVR	✓✓✓	–
			Fem-Fem	✓✓✓	–
			Bypass	✓✓✓✓	–

✓ Effectiveness	– Not effective or applicable	X Harmful

- Where the heat is applied (core or shell, internal or external, central or peripheral)
- Whether invasive or noninvasive
- Power requirements for the heat source (chemical, battery, 120 VAC)

Table 4-2 categorizes several heat sources according to these criteria and indicates their effectiveness, or potential for damage, in the treatment of hypothermia and frostbite.

With mild to moderate hypothermia, noninvasive heat sources are usually sufficient. However, a moderately to severely hypothermic individual placed in a 70° F (21° C) hospital room without an external heat source cannot produce enough heat to rewarm (Figure 4-5). External heat (active rewarming) is essential. Both invasive and noninvasive techniques have been developed.

Noninvasive techniques are preferable for stable individuals. Such techniques rewarm more slowly than invasive procedures, but most hypothermia victims have become cold slowly. The criterion for effective treatment is a steady rate of warming while maintaining full physiological control.

With severe hypothermia when cardiorespiratory activity is present, invasive measures such as arteriovenous fistula or body cavity lavage with warm fluids are warranted. If cardiac arrest has occurred, cardiopulmonary bypass is preferred.

NONINVASIVE TECHNIQUES

Currently, one of the easiest rewarming techniques employs a forced-air warming device, the Bair Hugger, commonly used to rewarm postoperative patients. Warm air blown into a warming cover exits through holes on the patient side of the cover and can provide convective heat transfer of 60 to 70 watts over the entire body. This technique has been found to increase core temperature by 4.3° F (2.4° C) per hour for nonshivering subjects and 5.9° F (3.3° C) per hour for shivering individuals (Figure 4-2). If the Bair Hugger blanket is not available, an ordinary blanket can be used but is less effective.

Further studies have been made with a collapsible rigid cover designed to take advantage of existing commercial heating units. When used for non-shivering, hypothermic volunteers, this cover has attenuated the afterdrop and resulted in more effective warming than occurs spontaneously. It can be used in any transport vehicle with a power inverter that produces 120 VAC and 10 amps.

HEATED IRRIGATION

Peritoneal lavage is accomplished through a tube inserted into one of the pelvic gutters through a minilaparoscopy incision, or over a guide wire previously inserted with a needle. Up to two liters (10 to 20 ml/kg) of heated normal saline, Ringer's lactate, or standard dextrose dialysate solution is infused, allowed to remain twenty to thirty minutes, and then aspirated. An exchange rate of 6 l/hr rewarms the core at 1.8° to 5.4° F (1° to 3° C) per hour. If adhesions are present, peritoneal lavage is less effective, is associated with more complications, and may not be possible. This technique has the advantage of providing some dialysis for drug overdose and rhabdomyolysis toxicity. Direct hepatic warming reactivates the metabolic functions of that organ. However, dialysis worsens hypokalemia, and electrolytes must be closely monitored.

Pleural (thoracic) lavage requires the placement of one or two large-bore thoracotomy tubes in one or both pleural spaces. One tube is placed anteriorly for installation of heated fluid. A second tube, if utilized, is placed posteriorly for drainage. If a second tube is not inserted, fluid instilled through the first tube must subsequently be aspirated. Only limited clinical studies have been reported, but rewarming rates as high as 5.4° to 10.8° F (3° to 6° C) have been achieved. This technique appears most suitable for rewarming during CPR. A tube in the left pleural cavity may precipitate fibrillation. Pleural adhesions greatly interfere with rewarming by this technique.

Mediastinal irrigation has been used following thoracotomy to warm a fibrillating, hypothermic heart. Electrical defibrillation may not be possible until the heart is warmed to about 86° F (30° C).

EXTRACORPOREAL REWARMING

Cardiopulmonary bypass rewarming is a valuable rewarming technique, particularly when spontaneous cardiac activity is absent and circulation must be restored promptly to avoid neurologic damage, or the heart must be rewarmed to allow electrical defibrillation. Femoral vein to femoral artery bypass that incorporates an oxygenator and heat exchanger is the technique of choice and avoids the complications of thoracotomy. A catheter inserted through the femoral vein into the right atrium to actively aspirate the venous return allows higher flow rates and improves decompression of the myocardium.

Rewarming rates of almost 18° F (10° C) per hour, or as high as 1.8° to 3.6° F (1° to 2° C) every three to five minutes, have been achieved. One of the disadvantages of bypass is the passage of fluid through endothelium damaged by hypothermia. Compartment pressures can be raised, and frostbite damage may be increased.

Continuous arteriovenous rewarming (CAVR) is another extracorporeal technique. Catheters are inserted into a femoral vein and the contralateral femoral artery, and blood is circulated from the arterial catheter, through a heat exchanger, and back into the femoral vein. Because perfusion pressure is provided by the individual's own cardiovascular system, a blood pressure of at least 60 mmHg must be present.

For venovenous rewarming, blood is removed from a vein, usually a large central vein, heated to 104° F (40° C), and returned through another catheter. In a modification of this technique the blood is heparinized, pumped through a heat exchanger, treated with protamine to neutralize the heparin, and returned through a subclavian or jugular vein to preferentially warm the heart.

Routine hemodialysis using a heat exchanger is another technique for extracorporeal blood rewarming. It is particularly useful for individuals with renal failure, electrolyte abnormalities, or intoxication with a dialyzable substance.

CHAPTER 5

Keep Your Head Up:
Cold Water Immersion

MANY RECREATIONAL, MILITARY, and commercial activities occur in, on, or over cold water. Whitewater rafting, scuba diving, swimming races, even fly fishing result in intentional immersion in cold water. Ocean kayaking, sailing, and commercial fishing present the possibility of accidental immersion. Cross-country skiing, snowmobiling, ice fishing, and similar activities sometimes require travel over ice that could break and leave the participant suddenly immersed in very cold water.

During filming of a cold water educational video in Alaska, a woman and a man were asked to swim as far as they could in 54° F (12° C) water. The woman, who was a good swimmer but was not wearing a personal flotation device (PFD), swam for only four minutes before failing and requiring rescue. The man was expected to swim much faster and farther because he was wearing a PFD. What happened was surprising. During the first few minutes the woman was swimming fairly smoothly, but the man was floundering badly, even though he was wearing a PFD. He was struggling so much that organizers thought he would have to be pulled out of the water. A few minutes later, however, after the woman could no longer swim, the man calmly swam by the boat and continued until the film crew became bored and ended the demonstration. When questioned about his early problems, the man said that he was shocked when he jumped into the water. He was breathing uncontrollably and flailing his arms around helplessly to keep his head above water. Finally, in a state of exhaustion, he gave up struggling and found that his PFD kept him afloat and he could relax. He got his breathing under control, rapidly regained his strength, and started swimming again, only this time calmly and efficiently. When pulled from the water he stated that he could have continued for quite awhile.

Cold water immersion is still poorly understood by the general public, and even by many outdoor medical experts. A common belief is that immersion in very cold water, even with protective clothing, results in death from hypothermia within minutes. A survey of almost five hundred medical, paramedical, and search and rescue professionals over a period of years found that only 5 percent understood that more than thirty minutes are required for individuals who fall into ice water while wearing winter clothing to become clinically hypothermic (Figure 5-1). These incorrect assumptions have serious implications because believing that death from hypothermia is imminent can result in panic and poor decision making, making a bad situation worse—even fatal. One unfortunate outcome of this erroneous belief is the fatalistic attitude of many commercial fishers that, even if a PFD is worn, they have no hope of survival if they accidentally fall overboard in cold water.

Although most cold water immersion fatalities do occur within less than twenty minutes, the deaths occur while the victims are still normothermic. Both of the Alaskan video demonstrators would have died within a few minutes if they had not been wearing PFDs and no one had been there to rescue them, but they would not have been hypothermic. This chapter describes how people die in cold water, and how applying this knowledge can increase their chance of survival.

Cold water has been defined as water with a temperature below 68° to 77° F (20° to 25° C). For this chapter an upper limit of 68° F (20° C) was chosen because water below this temperature poses a significant risk of hypothermia, and because many cold water survival predictions consider only water temperatures in this range. Finally, a distinction must be made between immersion, which refers to situations in which the head is out of the water and the individual is able to maintain an airway, and submersion, which refers to drowning scenarios in which the head is under water.

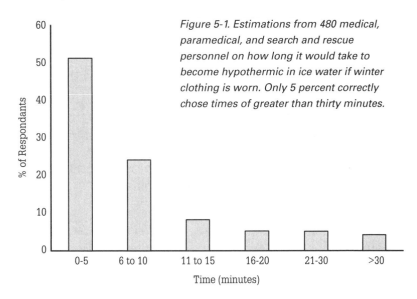

Figure 5-1. Estimations from 480 medical, paramedical, and search and rescue personnel on how long it would take to become hypothermic in ice water if winter clothing is worn. Only 5 percent correctly chose times of greater than thirty minutes.

THE FOUR STAGES OF COLD WATER IMMERSION

The reaction of human bodies to immersion in cold water has been divided into four stages:

Cold Shock is the initial reaction that can kill within seconds to two minutes by producing respiratory or cardiac problems that lead to drowning or sudden cardiac death.

Cold Incapacitation occurs within two to thirty minutes of immersion; it impairs physical performance and leads to an inability to self-help, swimming failure, and drowning.

Hypothermia develops after thirty minutes or more of immersion and progresses until shivering stops and the victim becomes unconscious. At this point, drowning occurs if the head is not supported above water; if the head does remain above water survival continues until the body core cools enough to result in cardiac standstill.

Circumrescue Collapse can occur just prior to, during, or minutes to several hours after rescue. The effects range from syncope (fainting) to cardiac standstill, and result from loss of arterial blood pressure, further cooling of the heart (afterdrop), or metabolic abnormalities.

Cold Shock

Sudden immersion in cold water stimulates one to several large inspiratory gasps, which may be followed by hyperventilation, and may also be associated with a substantial increase in blood pressure and heart rate. (If entry into the water includes complete submersion of the head, the gasp reflex can result in aspiration of water and immediate drowning.) Subsequent hyperventilation usually diminishes within seconds to minutes, but may be exaggerated and prolonged by emotional stress and panic. Uncontrolled hyperventilation can cause numbness, muscle weakness, or even fainting, which make coordinating breathing with swimming strokes very difficult, a complication that could easily lead to drowning. Cold shock can theoretically occur in water warmer than 68° F (20° C), although these effects are more life-threatening at temperatures below 59° F (15° C) and worsen as water temperature decreases. Healthy persons may succumb to cold shock as the result of uncontrolled respiratory responses; individuals with cardiac disease may experience cardiac arrest or ventricular fibrillation (Figure 5-2).

The best way to minimize cold shock is to enter cold water in a slow and controlled manner and, most importantly, to keep the head from being submersed. Individuals should focus on surviving the first minute: suppressing panic, and consciously getting breathing under control. Once breathing is controlled, individuals usually have adequate time to evaluate the situation and make proper survival choices.

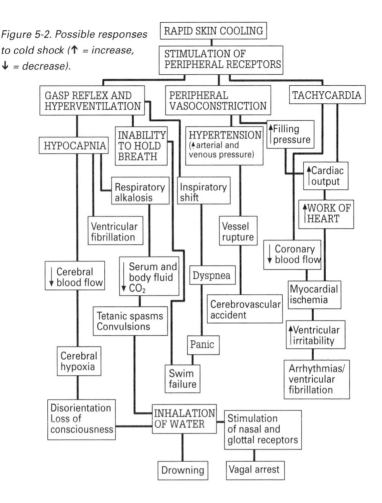

Figure 5-2. Possible responses to cold shock (↑ = increase, ↓ = decrease).

Cold Incapacitation

In addition to short-term cold shock, the body attempts to preserve a normal core temperature of 98.6° F (37° C) by decreasing heat loss and increasing heat production. Constriction of the blood vessels in the limbs shunts blood from the extremities to the core and decreases heat loss through the limbs, which allows limb tissues to cool rapidly. The intense cooling of muscle and nerve tissues results in muscular failure, and the individual progressively becomes incapacitated, losing the ability to swim, maintain posture in the water, or use the hands to perform other survival tasks. In water near 32° F (0° C) incapacitation can occur within two to ten minutes, but takes progressively longer at higher water temperatures. In a demonstration, the writer, while wearing a snowmobile suit in ice water, was completely incapacitated within six minutes after swimming only fifty feet.

Once physical strength and dexterity start to diminish, the trend continues and does not reverse itself. Therefore the best course of action must be determined promptly and followed in a timely manner. Such actions could include:

○ Escaping (pulling oneself out of the water, or inflating and boarding a life raft)

○ Minimizing exposure (getting as much of the body as possible out of the water and onto a floating object)

○ Ensuring flotation (if getting out of the water is not possible, putting on or inflating a PFD, or attaching oneself to an object above the water surface)

○ Attracting assistance (activating signaling devices)

Executing these actions while cold shock predominates may be difficult. However, once breathing is under control, immediate action should be taken. If self-rescue is not possible, actions to minimize heat loss should be initiated. In open water individuals should remain as still as possible in the Heat Escape Lessening Posture (HELP), in which arms are pressed against the chest and legs are pressed together, or huddling with other survivors, with each person pressing their legs together while forming a tight circle (Figure 5-3). If an individual has broken through the ice, arms should be placed up on the ice and legs pressed together. Drawstrings in clothing should be tightened to decrease the flow of cold water within clothing layers.

Hypothermia

The individual who survives the immediate and short-term phases of cold water immersion faces the possible onset of hypothermia because continuous heat loss eventually decreases core temperature. True clinical hypothermia only becomes a significant contributor to death if immersion lasts more than thirty minutes in ice water; this period lengthens as water temperature increases. The rate of core cooling depends on water temperature, the amount

H.E.L.P. (Heat Escape Lessening Posture)   Huddle

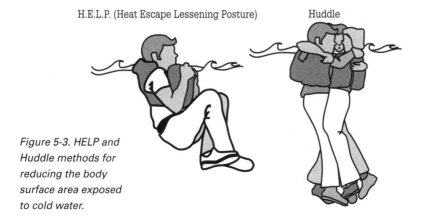

Figure 5-3. HELP and Huddle methods for reducing the body surface area exposed to cold water.

of the body that is immersed, metabolic heat production, body morphology, external insulation provided by clothing and survival gear, water turbulence and height of waves, behavior (amount of movement), and posture (HELP, or huddle). Figure 5-4 illustrates the way high body-fat content considerably extends survival time in cold water.

Even in ice-cold water, an hour or more may be required for a person to become unconscious due to hypothermia, if a PFD, flotation snowmobile suit, or some other device eliminates the need for vigorous exercise to keep from drowning. Once a victim is unconscious, another hour or more may be required for the heart to stop if the head is kept above water (a PFD is worn and the water is calm enough for waves not to wash over the mouth, or the arms are frozen to the ice).

ONE MINUTE—TEN MINUTES—ONE HOUR

The slogan "one minute—ten minutes—one hour" provides a simple way to remember the first three phases of cold water immersion and what to do during each of them to increase the chances of surviving. The time taken by these responses varies somewhat, but the estimates are approximately correct.

After falling into very cold water people have:

○ *1 minute to get breathing under control* (panic must be avoided!)

○ *10 minutes of useful movement* (time available to get out of the water or create a stable situation)

○ *1 hour before becoming unconscious due to hypothermia* (unnecessary movement or struggling should be avoided to decrease heat loss and widen the window of opportunity for rescue). A person wearing a PFD may have another hour until the heart is stopped by hypothermia.

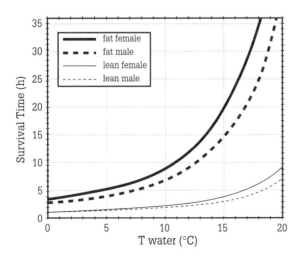

Figure 5-4. Predicted times to lethal hypothermia for unprotected immersion in rough water at different temperatures for tall, lean males (14.3% body fat) and females (19.0% body fat), and for short, fat males (28.1% body fat) and females (32.3% body fat).

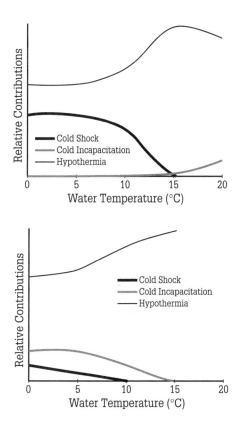

Figure 5-5. Estimation of the relative contributions of cold shock, cold incapacitation, and hypothermia to death in water at different temperatures. (Above: Estimation if no flotation is available. Below: Estimation if flotation is available.)

Figure 5-5 estimates the relative contributions of cold shock, cold incapacitation, and hypothermia to death as water temperature decreases from 68° to 32° F (20° to 0° C). This figure illustrates the importance of wearing a PFD. Without a flotation device, remaining afloat long enough to die from hypothermia is virtually impossible, and death occurs quickly from drowning as the result of cold shock or cold incapacitation. Wearing a PFD accomplishes two objectives: survival time is increased tremendously and the contributions of cold shock and cold incapacitation are decreased substantially.

Circumrescue Collapse

An estimated 20 percent of individuals recovered alive from cold water die as a result of circumrescue complications, either before, during, or within twenty-four hours after rescue. Prior to imminent rescue, mental relaxation and decreased output of stress hormones may cause a drop in blood pressure, resulting in fainting and drowning. The act of rescue may also cause sudden collapse. Pulling a person out of the water in a vertical position removes the hydrostatic squeeze on the body and lower limbs, allowing blood to pool in the extremities and causing decreased blood pressure. The extra cardiac work—or rough handling—may induce arrest or fibrillation of a cold heart.

Death may also occur within minutes to hours after rescue. A rescued individual may be severely compromised by acidic metabolic by-products accumulating in the extremities, a heart extremely prone to dysrhythmias, decreased or absent consciousness, and low blood volume. Sudden redistribution of blood to the extremities, particularly the lower extremities, may cause collapse as a result of decreased blood pressure, sudden return of metabolites to an irritable heart, or continued decrease in temperature (afterdrop) of an unstable heart. Core temperature continues to drop and the heart reacts with tachycardia (a high heart rate) or fibrillation. Finally, individuals often aspirate water during long periods of immersion, which may produce delayed lethal hypoxia because gas exchange in the lungs is compromised.

LONG-TERM SURVIVAL IN COLD WATER
Staying Alive

If a person survives the initial stages of cold water immersion, heat loss must be minimized, and energy must be conserved. The rate of body core cooling depends on water temperature, body size, and fatness. Large people cool more slowly than small people; fat people cool more slowly than thin people (Figure 5-4). Children cool more rapidly than adults. Activity also affects core cooling. Exercise heat production can almost never equal the increased heat loss to the water caused by increased peripheral blood flow and limb movement through cold water. Water has high heat conductivity and drains heat from the body approximately twenty-five times faster than air at the same temperature.

If no flotation is worn, valuable energy is lost keeping the head above water. Survival depends on swimming to safety or obtaining some other form of flotation. When swimming or treading water a person cools much faster than when remaining still, and cold incapacitation eventually results in swimming failure. Figure 5-6 illustrates how swimming increases heat loss from the skin in the area of exercising muscles.

Figure 5-6. Infrared thermograms indicating relative skin temperatures (and therefore relative heat loss):
(a) *before immersion in 45.5° F (7.5° C) water,*
(b) *after holding still in the water for fifteen minutes, and*
(c) *after swimming for fifteen minutes. Lighter areas are warmer.*

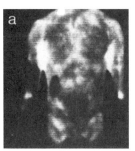
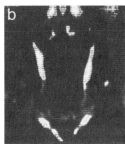
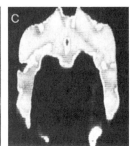

If a PFD is worn, it has the immediate benefit of maintaining a person's airway without the effort of swimming. It can keep a person afloat even when unconscious. An average-size person wearing light clothing and a PFD or life jacket may survive three to six hours in 50° F (10° C) water by remaining still. During cold water immersion more than 95 percent of the heat loss is to the water. Since most boats float even when capsized or swamped, getting into or onto the boat to get as far out of the water as possible is usually advisable. If the body cannot be raised out of the water, the Heat Escape Lessening Posture can be adopted.

A group of immersed individuals should keep together for psychological support and possibly for increased thermal insulation. The group may try to adopt a huddle position, but this position can be difficult to maintain in rough water because some in the group have their backs to the waves and movement through the water is limited. At the very least, victims should tether themselves together with ropes or straps and individually adopt the HELP position.

Several flotation or antiexposure suits are available. Some products, such as floater suits or antiexposure overalls, are worn continuously. Others, such as full dry suits with thermal liners, are more bulky and are put on when immersion is imminent. These products provide thermal protection over more of the body surface and can greatly extend cold water survival.

PFDs and flotation suits must be worn at all times. Thinking they can be put on in the water creates a false sense of security. In the water, particularly cold water, donning a PFD can be very difficult, and putting on a survival suit is almost impossible.

Signaling for Help

At sea, cold water immersion survivors should be prepared to use signals to draw the attention of search and rescue personnel. Signaling can be accomplished with devices or by actions. Signaling devices include dye markers and brightly colored streamers that can be seen from the air, as well as signal mirrors and flares that can be seen from the air and for several miles over water. The survivor can also increase visibility by waving the arms or lying backward and vigorously splashing the water with arms and legs. A group of survivors can face away from each other, lock their elbows together, and lay on their backs to form a star that can be seen easily from the air. If a search aircraft is nearby, visibility can be impressively increased if everyone kicks their legs vigorously.

To Swim or Not to Swim

The decision to swim or not is difficult. Distances on the water are very deceptive. Staying with a vessel is usually best because it makes spotting immersed individuals by rescuers easier. Even a capsized vessel is easier to see than a lone person in the water. Generally, individuals should not consider swimming unless they are very close to shore or a floating object, or they have little chance of rescue. One study showed that volunteers could swim for up to an hour in 50° F (10° C) water without a PFD. However, this time would decrease substantially at lower temperatures and caution should be used in estimating swimming ability, water temperature, and the distance to safety. Other recent studies have shown that individuals wearing PFDs were able to swim about 2,950 and 2,130 feet (900 and 650 meters) in 57° F (14° C) and 50° F (10° C) water. Survivors wearing PFDs can be more liberal in deciding to swim because flotation allows them to gradually make their way to safety and, in the worst case, they can still float if they become completely exhausted.

Finally, the decision whether to remain still or to exercise is affected by the amount of insulation that is worn. A full-coverage, insulated survival suit can prevent the excessive heat loss that usually occurs when an uninsulated person exercises in cold water. A recent study in a wave tank filled with ice water, demonstrated that five minutes of moderate leg exercise (cycling motions) every twenty minutes slows core cooling considerably, provides more physical comfort, and probably delays exhaustion from lack of energy substrate (Figure 5-7).

Figure 5-7. Core temperature profiles of volunteers in 35.6° F (2° C) water and 35.6° F (2° C) air. Volunteers were wearing neoprene survival suits and either lay still in the water (black diamonds) for three hours, or performed five minutes of leg cycle-like exercise every twenty minutes (white triangles). Intermittent exercise was more comfortable, reduced shivering, and decreased core cooling allowing volunteers to remain in the water for up to six hours.

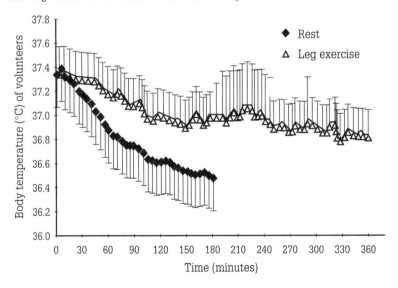

Falling Through the Ice

A person who has fallen through ice must not panic and should concentrate on controlling gasping and hyperventilation. The next step is to take time to move toward the strongest part of the ice, which is usually where the body was supported before breaking through. After putting the arms up on the ice as far as possible, the individual should flutter kick to bring the body to a horizontal position near the water surface, and while continuing to kick, should pull the body up on the ice with the hands and arms (Figure 5-8). At this point, rolling away from the hole and crawling to thicker ice before attempting to stand and walk is essential.

Cold water immersion is a problem that supports the axiom "an ounce of prevention is better than a pound of cure." Prevention requires training, equipment, and common sense.

Figure 5-8. Procedure for self-rescue after falling through ice.
Top two photos: *Victim does not panic but calmly places arms on the ice edge.*
Bottom left: *Victim kicks his legs until his body is horizontal at the water surface.*
Bottom right: *Victim kicks and pulls until his body is on top of the ice. The next step is to roll carefully away from the hole and crawl to safety.*

CHAPTER 6

I've Got That Sinking Feeling:
Cold Water Drowning

FEW MEDICAL REPORTS arouse as much excitement as the "miraculous survival" of individuals submersed under cold water for long periods. Anna fell down a waterfall gully while backcountry skiing and became wedged between rocks and overlying thick ice. The area was continuously flooded by icy water. She struggled for forty minutes before finally becoming unconscious. Another thirty-nine minutes were required for rescue personnel to extract her from beneath the ice. Her core temperature had dropped to 57° F (13.7° C), yet she lived. Anna currently holds the record for surviving with the lowest core temperature to result from accidental hypothermia/cold water drowning without any long-term neurological deficit.

Several advances have been made recently in the understanding of how individuals survive cold water submersion for extended periods with full or partial neurological recovery. The most important features in these unusual cases are low water temperature and subsequent brain cooling, as well as redistribution of blood flow, which redirects the diminishing oxygen supply to the brain.

MECHANISMS OF COOLING

The protective effect of brain cooling depends on the core (and brain) temperature at the cessation of oxygen delivery, and the subsequent rate and extent of the decrease in that temperature. Since the early 1960s surgeons have taken advantage of the first of these two principles—initial low brain temperature—by using cardiopulmonary bypass to cool neurosurgical patients to core temperatures as low as 48° F (9° C), which allows arrest of brain blood flow for at least fifty-five minutes with full neurologic recovery (Figure 6-1).

Since core temperature is likely to be near normal at the onset of an accidental submersion, the second principle—rapid cooling after the onset of anoxia (absence of oxygen)—becomes significant. Children have a greater surface-area-to-mass ratio than adults, which results in greater relative conductive heat loss and increased rates of core cooling. This mechanism is often cited as support for the belief that children have a survival advantage

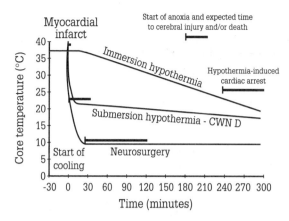

Figure 6-1. Times to cerebral injury or death after the sudden onset of anoxia. Examples include anoxia induced by myocardial infarction at normal core temperature, hypothermia-induced cardiac arrest during immersion hypothermia, loss of air supply after cold water drowning, and electrically induced arrest after protective cooling for neurosurgery. The times are representative; actual survival times may vary.

over adults in cold water submersion. However, the perceived survival advantage may be skewed by the higher propensity of children to drown. Several adult drownings with prolonged submersion followed by intact survival are reviewed in this chapter.

Whether surface conductive heat loss alone can cause enough core cooling to provide cerebral protection from anoxia is doubtful. During a drowning study conducted on shaved, anesthetized dogs immersed or submersed in cold water (38° F [4° C]) core temperatures decreased 5° F (3° C) within four minutes in control dogs that were immersed with their heads out of the water. However, when dogs were completely submersed, core temperature dropped much more (20° F [11° C]) in the same amount of time. Why did the totally submersed dogs cool so much more? Surprisingly, these mammals continued to breathe water for four minutes following submersion; their breathing rate transiently increased from twenty to sixty breaths per minute, and then fell to approximately ten breaths per minute. Cardiac activity also continued during submersion as the heart rate fell steadily from 120 to 40 beats per minute after four minutes. Body weight and blood measurements such as hematocrit and osmolality indicated that water was actually inhaled and absorbed by the submersed dogs and the rapid cooling was produced by convective heat exchange in the lung. Dogs immersed with their heads out of the water were cooled only by surface conduction, and their core temperatures did not drop as much. Repeated inhalation of cold water into the lungs effectively cools the blood, which cools the brain.

Although these dog studies have clearly demonstrated continued ventilation of cold water after submersion, this response in humans has not been reliably documented. However, reaching the "struggle phase" of breath holding (see below), during which involuntary breathing movements predominate, coupled with unconsciousness, would be expected to result in inhalation of water, at least under some circumstances. Experimental and anecdotal evidence in humans is rare. However, one helicopter crash survivor reported that, after being trapped underwater for some time, he recalled feeling he was about to die and that he was breathing water in and out just prior to escaping the cockpit. One of the determinants of cold water drowning survival is thought to be whether cold water is ventilated.

REDIRECTING LIMITED OXYGEN SUPPLY TO THE BRAIN

The dive reflex is elicited in diving mammals by contact of the face with cold water. It consists of breath holding, intense peripheral vasoconstriction, decreased heart rate, decreased cardiac output, and increased blood pressure (hypertension). Breath holding delays drowning and provides an oxygen reservoir in the lungs. Selective vasoconstriction and progressive hypertension ensure that the heart and brain, which are most important for survival, are adequately oxygenated at the expense of less sensitive organs and muscles.

The effectiveness of this reflex, especially the breath-holding response, in humans is equivocal. Hayward immersed adults suddenly in water ranging from 32° to 95° F (0° to 35° C) and found that colder water actually decreased breath holding duration. The reduced breath-holding response would actually promote drowning.

In a second study, children four to thirteen years old and adults twenty to sixty-eight years old were immersed in 84° F (29° C) water. Breath-holding duration was shorter in the children than adults, decreased progressively as the children got younger (to ten seconds in four-year-olds), and would be expected to be even shorter in colder water. This led the authors to conclude, "These findings do not support the postulate that the dive response has an important role in the enhanced resuscitability associated with cold water drowning, thereby shifting emphasis to hypothermia as the mechanism for this phenomenon."

In other studies, significant breath-holding duration—up to 150 seconds with facial immersion in 50° F (10° C) water—has been demonstrated in active breath-hold divers. Interestingly, voluntary breath holding consists of two phases. The first, or "easy phase," is not associated with breathing movements. However, increasing arterial carbon dioxide levels reach a physiological breakpoint and begin to stimulate respiratory movements, so that during the second, or "struggle phase," progressive involuntary breathing movements do occur.

Although humans do not increase breath holding in cold water, the cardiovascular elements of the dive reflex do seem active. In one study, facial submersion in cold water stimulated a slow heart rate (bradycardia) that was inversely proportional to water temperature; heart rate was reduced by about eighteen beats per minute in 50° F (10° C) water. Bradycardia and peripheral vasoconstriction redirect the limited blood and oxygen supply to the heart and brain. Therefore, individuals with a more active dive reflex may have some advantage during cold water submersion.

PROTECTION FROM ANOXIA BY COOLING

Anoxic protection provided by cerebral cooling is attributed to decreased cerebral metabolic requirements for oxygen, which would be halved if tissue temperature decreased 18° F (10° C). The human brain can survive anoxia for only about five minutes at normal body temperatures. However, Michenfelder demonstrated diminished cerebral requirements for oxygen after cooling to 81° F (27° C) and 63° F (17° C) that would allow the brain to survive anoxic insult for fifteen and seventy-two minutes. Additional mechanisms are required to explain intact survival after prolonged submersion of individuals with core temperatures above 86° F (30° C).

Over the past decade several studies directed at protecting the brain during or following events such as heart attacks and strokes have demonstrated that even moderate brain cooling provides substantial cerebral protection from lack of oxygen. Moderate cooling of rat brains to 95° F (35° C) and 91° F (33° C) greatly reduces or even eliminates neuronal damage caused by ten to twenty minutes of totally absent blood flow. The response to electrical stimulation and performance in a maze are much better when ten minutes of absent circulation occurs at a brain temperature of 86° F (30° C) than when temperature is normal.

When the brain cools only 5° to 9° F (3° to 5° C), it is protected more than would be predicted from decreased oxygen demand alone. The extra protection relates to changes in neurotransmitter release and other factors in the cold brain. Furthermore, even though the mammalian dive reflex has limited effectiveness in humans, any cold-induced circulatory adjustments would favor conservation of oxygen for the heart and brain. Finally, cold water ventilation could accelerate brain cooling and provide further protection.

These conclusions are supported by some adult case reports. Three individuals aged twenty-one to thirty-one years who were accidentally submersed for seventeen to twenty-five minutes were admitted to the hospital with rectal temperatures ranging from 73° to 90° F (23° to 32° C). All were resuscitated and rewarmed successfully. For each of these individuals, submersion times were almost double (triple in one person) the survival times predicted by the temperature/cerebral oxygen requirement relationship.

The skier described at the beginning of this chapter encountered several conditions that helped her survive and go on to complete her training as a physician. Brain cooling is necessary for surviving such a long period of anoxia. As stated earlier, however, protection is based on not only the degree of brain cooling but also the speed of cooling. Anna was in an unusual situation because her face was in an air pocket that allowed her to continue breathing for her first forty minutes in ice water. During this time she became very hypothermic. As a result her brain was already cold when she became unconscious and drowned, which helped her survive such a long subsequent period of anoxia.

EVALUATION AND TREATMENT

As much as possible, a drowning victim should be kept in a horizontal position during removal from the water. The head or neck should not be moved if a neck injury is a possibility. Full resuscitative efforts should be administered for any person who has been submersed in cold (less than 68° F or 20° C) water for less than one hour; although successful resuscitation is much more likely at water temperatures below 50° F (10° C). If a person has been submersed in water of any temperature for more than one hour, resuscitation efforts are usually unsuccessful, and need not be started. If the submersion time is unknown, it should be considered to have been less than one hour unless there are obvious signs of long submersion, such as slippage of skin or animal predation.

Unlike individuals with hypothermia, the major problem for individuals who have drowned in cold water is lack of oxygen for the brain rather than low temperature of the heart, and providing oxygen is the primary concern. The airway should be cleared with any of the standard maneuvers, but abdominal or chest thrusts should not be administered unless evidence of a solid, foreign-body airway obstruction is present. Pulse and respirations should be checked for up to sixty seconds. If they cannot be detected, CPR should be started immediately. If a defibrillator is available and the patient is in ventricular fibrillation, one series of defibrillation attempts should be performed. If defibrillation is successful, the person should be transported to the nearest medical facility immediately. In areas where cardiopulmonary bypass is readily available, transporting the drowned person to a facility with these capabilities should be considered. Bypass addresses both of the individual's primary medical problems by oxygenating and warming the blood (Figure 6-2).

Because severe hypothermia (core temperature below 82° F [28° C]) is rare in cold water drowning, hypothermia is less critical than the cardiac, pulmonary, or coagulation abnormalities. Rewarming is generally delayed until arrival at the hospital, and its primary purpose is raising the heart temperature to make defibrillation more effective. A low blood volume is rarely a problem in cold water drownings; therefore a balanced salt solution should be infused at a "keep open" rate.

Any person who has been submerged and unconscious should be transported to a hospital, even if he or she has regained consciousness. Accumulation of fluid in the lungs (noncardiogenic pulmonary edema) may develop six to twenty-four hours after submersion and the individual could die as the result of inadequate gas exchange in the lung. Continued monitoring is essential during this period.

Figure 6-2. Cold water drowning treatment algorithm based on State of Alaska Cold Injuries Guidelines

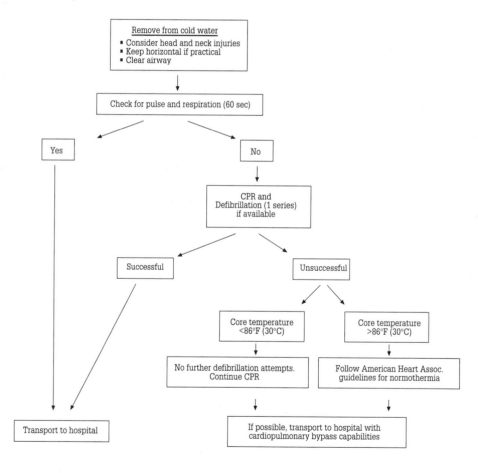

CHAPTER 7

You're As Cold As Ice:
Frostbite

FROSTBITE IS A LOCALIZED cold injury produced by freezing. This injury is almost always limited to the upper and lower extremities or to smaller structures such as the ears or nose. The hands and feet do not contain large heat-producing muscles and are a considerable distance from the major sites of heat generation. Furthermore, their blood supply is the first to be reduced when the body needs to conserve heat.

The toes are the most common site of frostbite, but the rest of the foot frequently is involved also. During outdoor activities in cold weather, shoes or boots may be in contact with ice or snow, subjecting the feet to conductive heat loss as well as the radiant, convective, and evaporative heat loss that the rest of the body experiences. The fingers and hands are also common sites of frostbite and can suffer severe cold exposure if gloves or mittens are removed.

Minor frostbite injuries may also involve other tissues, such as the ears and tip of the nose. These structures are thin, easily chilled, and often exposed directly to wind. The resulting injuries are rarely severe and are sometimes referred to as frostnip.

Two other contributors to frostbite of the hands and feet reduce the blood supply, and therefore heat delivery, to those tissues. The first is obstruction of the blood supply to the extremities by constricting clothing. The most common offenders are tightly laced boots and crampons. The second contributor is hypothermia, which causes constriction of the peripheral blood vessels in an effort to conserve heat for the body core.

Contact with cold metal can produce very rapid freezing of tissues because metal is such an excellent conductor of heat. Injuries of this type have been experienced by most people through contact with metal ice cube trays, car door handles, or mailboxes at subfreezing temperatures. Deeper frostbite is possible from prolonged contact with larger objects, such as wrenches or jack handles.

Organic liquids, such as gasoline, or solvents that have been left outdoors in below-freezing weather can also produce severe injuries. These fluids remain liquid at temperatures far below the freezing temperature of water. When they contact tissues, such supercooled liquids absorb so much heat from these tissues they cause almost instantaneous freezing.

Frostbite only occurs at temperatures below freezing, but the actual temperature and time of exposure can vary considerably. Of 812 U.S. Army frostbite victims during the Korean conflict, 80 percent were injured at temperatures between -0.4° and 18.5° F (-18° and -7.5° C), and only 10 percent were injured at lower temperatures. Of all the victims, 67 percent had been immobilized by enemy fire, sleeping in a foxhole, or riding in a truck. Thirteen percent of the injuries occurred after less than seven hours of exposure, 68 percent within seven to twelve hours, 10 percent within thirteen to eighteen hours, and 9 percent occurred after eighteen hours of exposure.

PREDISPOSITION TO FROSTBITE

A number of studies carried out by military physicians have demonstrated an increased susceptibility to localized cold injury for certain groups of individuals. For example, African-Americans are three to six times more susceptible to frostbite than Caucasians because members of this ethnic group do not increase their heat production as efficiently: they begin shivering at lower core temperatures. African-Americans tend to have long, thin fingers and toes, as well as thin arms and legs, that do not conserve heat well. Their fingers cool faster when immersed in cold water, reach a lower temperature before rewarming begins (the Lewis hunting reaction), and do not rewarm as much as those of Caucasians. The greater susceptibility of African-Americans to frostbite possibly is a result of long residence in tropical climates, where heat dissipation is more essential than heat conservation.

Other evidence of a genetic predisposition to cold injury is that the incidence of frostbite is higher than expected in Caucasians with type O blood and lower than expected in individuals with type A or type B blood.

Regardless of ethnicity, soldiers stationed in Alaska who were born in the southern part of the United States have an incidence of frostbite almost four times higher than soldiers born in northern states. Moreover, individuals who had already spent one winter in Alaska had a lower incidence of frostbite than newcomers. Presumably, these differences result from greater experience in dealing with a cold environment, but cold accommodation likely played some role; decreased vasoconstriction response would leave fingers and toes warmer and less likely to become frostbitten.

Lower military rank and educational level also are associated with a higher incidence of frostbite. Smokers have a higher incidence of frostbite than nonsmokers, presumably due to the vasoconstrictive effect of nicotine. Individuals who have previously suffered a cold injury have a greater risk of subsequent injury, but the reason is not clear because the second injury often involves a different part of the body.

Higher altitudes have been associated with a greater incidence of frostbite. Part of the increase is caused by the colder temperatures encountered at such elevations, but the hypoxia associated with altitude also diminishes resistance to cold injury. A reduction in cold-induced vasodilation at high altitudes has been demonstrated in individuals who are not native inhabitants of such elevations. The reduced vasodilation persisted even after acclimatization.

MECHANISMS OF TISSUE INJURY

The tissue injury resulting from frostbite is produced in two ways. The most obvious is actual freezing of the tissues. Although ice crystals form between the cells and grow by extracting water from them, the cells are physically disrupted by the ice crystals only to a limited extent (Figure 7-1). The dehydration and osmotic and chemical imbalances resulting from extraction of water from within the cell injure them, but permanent damage may be small. Under highly specific laboratory conditions frozen cells not only can survive for long periods of time but also can grow in an appropriate cell culture medium after thawing. (Ice crystal formation within the cells, which would be much more destructive, requires much faster freezing than usually occurs with frostbite.)

The second mechanism of tissue injury by frostbite, which is much more significant, is loss of the blood supply to the tissues. Blood may flow through larger vessels (one of the signs of adequate rewarming is a flushing of the frozen area), but oxygen cannot be delivered to the tissues because the small blood vessels that would carry it have been lost (Figures 7-2 and 7-3).

Figure 7-1. Ice formation in tissue during slow freezing: (1) Ice starts to form in the intracellular space. (2) The extracellular solution is concentrated because

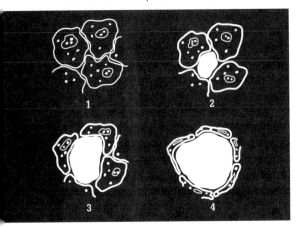

the water is frozen, and the resultant high osmotic pressure in the extracellular fluid forces intracellular water to diffuse through the cell wall, causing the cells to shrink. (3) Continuous growth of extracellular ice exerts mechanical pressure on cells, compressing them and causing more cell dehydration. (4) Dehydration causes significant damage to the cells.

Figure 7-2. Vasculature of rat paw before (top) and after (bottom) freezing. The abundant microvasculature that exists before freezing is destroyed and absent after freezing. However, after freezing large vessels remain intact and blood can still flow through the tissue, although the oxygen transfer capacity is destroyed.

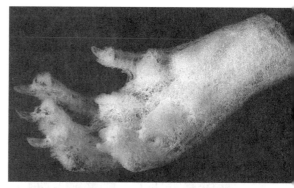

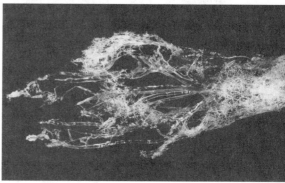

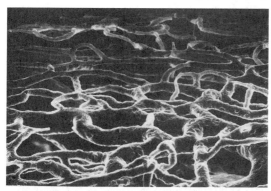

Figure 7-3. Scanning electron microscopy of vasculature before (top) and after (bottom) freezing. The microvascular capillaries that are present before freezing are absent after freezing.

All photographs this page courtesy of Murray Hamlet

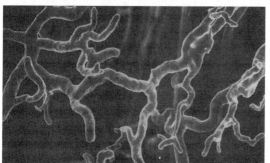

Additionally, the endothelial cells lining the surviving capillaries and small veins in frostbitten tissues are damaged by the cold in such a manner that they allow the liquid part of the blood (serum) to leak out into the tissues. Loss of this fluid diminishes the volume of the blood to such an extent that the rate of flow is greatly reduced. The blood cells no longer can remain suspended in the small volume of slowly moving serum and settle out or "sludge" within the vessels. Eventually the sludged blood clots, further obstructing the flow of blood, and circulation to the tissues ceases entirely.

Obstruction of the circulation by the sludging and subsequent clotting of blood plays a larger role in producing irreversible tissue damage than freezing. The changes produced in severely frostbitten tissues are identical to the damage caused by obstruction of the circulation by trauma or diseases such as arteriosclerosis (hardening of the arteries). More recently, analyses of the fluid within the blisters that develop after frostbitten tissues are thawed have disclosed the presence of significant quantities of substances that promote clotting, such as prostaglandin F2α and thromboxane B2, which are released from damaged endothelial cells. Other changes consistent with reperfusion injury occur with the appearance of arachidonic acid metabolites and oxygen free radicals.

The circulation of blood to frostbitten extremities is usually severely impaired before frostbite occurs because the blood vessels are strongly constricted to conserve body heat. Indeed, such vasoconstriction can be so marked that circulation to the fingers or toes almost ceases. Nonetheless, cold tends to protect the tissues from the effects of the diminished blood supply because the metabolism in the cells is so greatly reduced. In contrast, after thawing the cells are warm, metabolically active, and desperately in need of a good blood supply. An impaired blood supply at that time—which is typical—would be far more damaging.

PREVENTION

In an environment in which the temperature is below freezing, the only way to prevent frostbite is to wear protective clothing that keeps the entire body warm and protects the feet and hands.

Obstruction of the circulation must be avoided. Boots must not be laced too tightly; crampon straps must be loosened during rest periods; encircling, tightly fitting clothing must not be worn.

Cigarette smoking—in fact, nicotine from any source—constricts the peripheral blood vessels and tends to aggravate local cold injuries. Alcohol tends to dilate blood vessels and might help prevent frostbite, but alcohol abuse is one of the most common elements predisposing to frostbite because people do such stupid things under the influence of alcohol. (Exposure to severely cold conditions, such as immersion in cold water, overcomes the vasodilation produced by moderate amounts of alcohol, and the blood vessels constrict.) Nicotine and alcohol should be avoided in environments cold enough to produce cold injuries.

Frostbite of the ears and nose can be avoided by keeping those areas covered and out of the wind, particularly while on a moving vehicle such as a snowmobile, or during fast skiing. Frostbite of the corneas of the eyes, a rare injury produced by exposure of the eyes to cold air while moving rapidly, is treatable only by corneal transplantation. It can be prevented by wearing protective goggles.

DIAGNOSIS

The earliest symptom of frostbite is pain in the involved tissues. (If the tissues are rewarmed at this time, permanent injury can be avoided.) The next symptom is usually numbness. Sensory nerve conduction ceases at tissue temperatures below 45° F (7° C), and numbness is a sign that tissue freezing is imminent. As the tissue freezes, all sensation is lost and the pain disappears. This anesthesia may not be noticed by persons involved in an activity such as climbing that claims all of their attention. Frostbite victims, aware only that the pain is gone, may think their condition has improved, particularly if they are not thinking clearly as the result of hypothermia or altitude hypoxia. If environmental conditions have not changed, the disappearance of pain or numbness does not mean things are getting better, it means they are getting worse.

However, the symptoms produced by frostbite are variable. Some individuals never experience pain; a few never lose it. A clear head and awareness of conditions that threaten frostbite are essential for its early recognition.

Frostbitten tissues are usually pale because the blood vessels are constricted and the amount of blood in the tissues is reduced. Frostbite of the nose or ears may be first noticed by someone other than the victim because the pallor can be seen. However, color changes in the hands or feet usually go unnoticed because they are covered.

Frostbitten tissues also are usually firm or hard, although such changes may be limited to the superficial tissues. Sensation is typically absent in the involved tissues, particularly when the area is more than 1 inch (2.5 cm) in diameter.

If a large area, such as an entire foot or hand, is frostbitten, the tissues may appear purple as the result of sludging of blood. Such discoloration is an ominous finding that presages a loss of much—or all—of that portion of the extremity.

TREATMENT

The treatment for frostbite consists of rewarming the frozen tissues and minimizing the circulatory impairment that follows thawing.

Rewarming

The preferred treatment for frostbite is rapid rewarming in a water bath at a temperature between 99° to 102 °F (37° to 39° C). Slow rewarming is associated with significantly greater tissue damage than rapid rewarming and should be avoided if possible. Rubbing the frostbitten tissues with snow or similar cold therapy was advocated during the Napoleonic campaigns because rapid rewarming by campfires or similar sources of dry heat had produced so much devastation. However, cold therapy is now known to aggravate the injury and must not be used. Dry heat from engine exhausts, open fires, or similar sources cannot be controlled. Excessively high temperatures are usually produced, resulting in a combined burn and frostbite, a devastating injury that leads to far greater tissue loss. Finally, frozen tissues should not be rubbed. Even though rubbing produces heat through friction, it causes significant tissue damage because the embedded ice crystals rub against fragile cells.

Rewarming of frostbitten feet should not be carried out in situations—such as a high altitude snowfield—from which an individual can only escape by walking. Once frostbitten feet have thawed, the person is unable to walk on them and has to be carried.

No rewarming should be attempted until the victim has been evacuated to a situation in which there is no longer a significant possibility that the extremity might be refrozen. Thawing and refreezing does far more damage than walking on a frozen extremity.

Ideal situations for rapid rewarming are infrequently encountered before reaching a hospital. In urban surroundings frostbite victims are usually taken into a warm house until they can be transported to a hospital in a warm vehicle. By the time they reach the hospital the frostbitten tissues have thawed—slowly. Even in a large city the typical delay before obtaining help is twelve to seventy-two hours.

In mountaineering situations a person with frostbite often must walk down below the snow line to reach a base camp or similar facility where rapid rewarming can be carried out. Frostbitten tissues often have thawed by the time the individual gets there.

Ideally, rewarming of frostbitten areas should not be carried out until the person can be warmed to a normal body temperature and then be kept warm for as long as is required for recovery. When the body is cold, the blood vessels in the extremities are constricted. Rewarming frostbitten extremities in such circumstances would leave badly injured tissues without an adequate blood supply at the time it is most needed. Also, adequate facilities for rapid rewarming, including abundant supplies of warm water and methods for maintaining the temperature of the water bath, must be available.

If optimal facilities are not available, rapid rewarming is still indicated to limit tissue damage, keeping in mind that if the subject's toes or feet are thawed, the person must be carried to a point where motorized transportation is available.

For rewarming, any clothing or constricting items that could impair circulation, such as watchbands or rings, must be removed. The injured body part should be suspended in the center of the bath and not permitted to rest against the side or bottom.

The water bath should be maintained at a temperature between 99° and 102° F (37° and 39° C) and the water should be gently stirred. Warmer water would be more painful, does not improve prognosis, and may even cause burn injury if the water is too hot. The water must not be hot enough to feel uncomfortable to an uninjured person's hand. A large water bath permits more accurate control of the temperature and may warm the frozen extremity more rapidly, possibly resulting in less tissue loss.

A frostbitten hand or foot, like a block of ice, cools the water bath in which it is placed. The temperature of the bath must be maintained by adding warm water, not by heating the container. The victim's injured hand or foot could come in contact with the site to which heat was being applied and, because the tissues would be unable to feel the heat, a burn could result. The combination of frostbite and a burn is devastating. The injured extremity should be removed from the bath when hot water is being added and should not be returned until the water has been thoroughly mixed and the temperature checked. Warming usually requires twenty to forty minutes and should be continued until the frozen tissues are soft and pliable and the skin looks flushed.

Frostbitten tissues often become quite painful during rewarming. Aspirin or acetaminophen—alone or combined with codeine—or morphine, meperidine, or similar strong analgesics may be administered to help control the pain. Some individuals do not experience severe pain during rewarming, and for most the pain abates shortly afterwards.

Therapy to Improve Circulation

Since inadequacy of the blood supply to the frostbitten tissues appears to be responsible for much of the damage that results, efforts have been made to devise forms of therapy that would improve the circulation. Investigators who have found increased quantities of thromboxane and prostaglandins in the fluid of blisters that develop after rewarming have suggested that aspirin would inhibit the release of these agents. This therapy still needs further controlled study to confirm its effectiveness, but the treatment is so simple, and significant side effects are so uncommon, that it appears to be worth trying in a wilderness situation. It consists of simply administering aspirin—common, ordinary aspirin. One or two tablets should be given while the tissues are still frozen and every six hours thereafter. (More of this drug may commonly be needed to help control pain.)

Other forms of treatment that have been tried are directed toward eliminating blood vessel constriction in the frostbitten tissues. Smooth muscle in the walls of blood vessels is under the control of the autonomic (involuntary) nervous system. The sympathetic nerves, one of the two major components of the autonomic nervous system, cause the muscle to contract and constrict the blood vessels. (Parasympathetic nerves cause the muscles to relax and allow the vessels to dilate.) In experimental studies, cutting the sympathetic nerves to the frostbitten extremity has been found to modestly improve the outcome. However, such therapy is totally out of the question outside of a hospital.

Additional Measures

After rewarming, the patient must be kept warm, and the injured tissues must be elevated and carefully protected from trauma or irritation. Sterile gauze or cotton should be placed between frostbitten fingers or toes to absorb moisture. Some type of frame should hold sleeping bags or bedclothes off frostbitten feet. Unless frostbitten tissues have been injured beyond recovery, large blisters develop on them after rewarming. Keeping the blisters intact reduces the risk of infection.

Usually the victim should be evacuated immediately. Healing requires weeks or months, depending upon the extent of the injury. Even more time is required to regain full use of the extremity, if such is possible. The only exceptions would be individuals with very minor cold injuries.

During prolonged evacuation—such as on a long expedition—everything possible to prevent infection should be done. Cleanliness of the frostbitten area is vitally important. Soaking the extremity each day in disinfected, lukewarm water to which a germicidal soap has been added is helpful. Antibiotics probably should not be given routinely, but if infection appears to be present, and the patient is not allergic to penicillin, a broad spectrum antibiotic such as the combination of amoxicillin and clavulanate known as Augmentin or one of the quinolones, levofloxacin (Levaquin), ciprofloxacin (Cipro), or ofloxacin (Floxin), should be administered every six hours until a physician's care is obtained. Movement of the injured area should be encouraged, but should be limited to movements that can be performed voluntarily and without manipulation. Cigarette smoking or use of other tobacco products should be strictly prohibited because it further reduces the already deficient blood supply to the injured tissues.

Frostbite victims commonly suffer significant emotional reactions because they are faced with a long recovery, often with permanent disability. Continuing reassurance and emotional support are a significant part of their nursing care.

PROGNOSIS

The severity of frostbite injuries is notoriously difficult to judge during the early stages. Such determinations are essentially impossible while the tissues are still frozen. Every physician who has cared for a significant number of frostbite victims has been surprised by tissue loss that has been greater or less—usually the latter—than expected. Even after thawing the extent of the injury can not be determined accurately. Purple discoloration of an entire hand or foot—instead of pallor—is usually a sign of severe damage.

Following rewarming, several predictive signs appear. Rewarmed tissues develop a flushed appearance as the circulation is restored. Failure of the flush to appear or to extend to the tips of fingers or toes indicates that circulation has not been restored to those areas and they probably cannot be saved.

Minor frostbite—frostnip—of the tips of digits, ears, or nose may not result in blisters after rewarming. The tissues may just turn red for a few days, although a crust may form and the superficial layer of skin may be lost (Figure B in color insert).

Over areas of moderate frostbite blisters appear within about twelve to twenty-four hours after rewarming. Blisters filled with clear fluid that extend to the tips of the digits indicate the underlying tissues probably will recover (Figure C in color insert). Blisters filled with bloody fluid, blisters that do not extend to the tips of digits, or the failure of blisters to appear at all indicate that tissues are probably damaged beyond recovery (Figures D through G in color insert).

After a week or longer, dead frostbitten tissues develop a thick gray, dark green, or black covering—an eschar—that closely resembles the covering that develops over a third degree burn. In the ensuing weeks, fingers, toes, or other tissues that have been damaged beyond repair become black and mummified. Digits in such condition may separate or break off without surgery.

Radiologic examination of frostbitten tissues in the days or weeks following injury rarely discloses features that allow the extent of injury to be determined. Radionuclide scans hold promise of delineating early the tissues that ultimately will survive, but those studies are still in an investigational stage.

SURGICAL THERAPY

Many physicians who care for patients with frostbite recount horror stories about individuals who have avoided major hand or foot amputations only because they refused to allow surgeons to perform them, and subsequently have lost only fingers or toes—or the tips of those digits. Surgical amputation of frostbitten digits or extremities is almost never necessary until six weeks or more after injury. Only then is the extent of tissue death clearly demarcated. "Frozen in January—amputate in July" is a time-proven adage.

Even at that time, amputation should be limited to tissues that are clearly nonviable. Above knee or below knee amputations of legs following ischemic gangrene of one or more toes is usually necessary because the blood supply to the extremities is so impaired by arteriosclerosis that more distal amputation wounds do not heal. Such conditions do not prevail following frostbite. (Slightly higher amputations of feet may be necessary in order to construct stumps suitable for prostheses.)

Surgical intervention might be necessary to aid in the control of infection. Incision or excision of the eschar, not amputation, is all that is usually needed in such circumstances. If the lower extremity is frozen for a great length of time, the patient may develop a compartment syndrome, most commonly in the anterior tibial compartment and the foot. If compartment pressures are greater than 37 to 40 mmHg, the skin may need to be split or the patient may require a fasciotomy. Under these conditions a delay in performing the fasciotomy can be disastrous.

Surgery also may be needed for functional reconstruction of damaged extremities, primarily hands, after the dead tissues have separated.

CHAPTER 8

Don't Get Cold Feet:
Trench Foot

TRENCH FOOT IS A LOCALIZED cold injury that occurs most commonly in foot soldiers, although this disorder is occasionally encountered in civilians, particularly among the homeless. It was first described during the Napoleonic campaigns, though it must have been observed long before, and received its name during World War I from the men who spent weeks with their feet in cold water that flooded the trenches. During that conflict, the British had over 115,000 casualties with trench foot and frostbite.

During World War II, the Americans had approximately 60,000 trench foot casualties, 85 percent of them among infantry rifle companies. Only 15 percent of the casualties eventually returned to combat. During the worst part of the harsh 1944–45 winter, particularly during the German counter-offensive known as the Battle of the Bulge, trench foot accounted for one-third of the battlefield casualties admitted to general hospitals in the Paris area.

Identical injuries among victims of sea warfare, who spent days with their feet in the cold water of cramped, partially flooded lifeboats and life rafts, led to the name immersion foot.

Trench foot remains a devastating injury for soldiers in cold, wet weather. In the Falkland Islands war, 70 of the 516 British battle casualties requiring hospitalization were victims of trench foot. Estimates of the number who had significant injuries but did not require hospitalization ranged as high as two thousand. None of the British casualties required immediate amputation, an indication of the early and excellent care they received on the hospital ships. Reportedly, the Argentinean forces, which did not have such medical facilities available, had a far larger number of trench foot injuries and many amputations.

PREVENTION

Trench foot can be prevented by avoiding wet feet in a cold environment for prolonged periods of time. During World War I, the British dropped their rate of cold injury from 33.9 cases per thousand men in 1914 to 3.8 cases per thousand in 1918 by implementing three simple rules. Every soldier was required to have a spare pair of socks; arrangements for drying and reissue of socks during tours in the trenches were mandatory; and boots and socks had to be removed, the feet dried and massaged well (to promote circulation), and dry socks put on as circumstances allowed. Officers were charged with the responsibility for enforcing the preventive measures in their units.

Of course, during active combat avoiding being shot is undoubtedly more pressing than caring for wet feet. In some battlefield situations drying the feet or any part of the body may be impossible. However, awareness of the potential for disabling injury from prolonged exposure to wet and cold should lead officers, and the men for whom they are responsible, to take preventive measures whenever an opportunity can be found. Simply putting on dry socks and drying the boots as well as possible helps avoid trench foot or at least greatly reduces its severity.

In recent years a number of homeless individuals, who have no clean, dry socks, and no place to warm and dry their feet, have presented with typical trench foot.

Outdoor enthusiasts who are not in combat should rarely if ever have their feet wet and cold for days at a time. Fishermen, waterfowl hunters, white-water enthusiasts, and high-altitude climbers wearing vapor-impermeable boots appear to be at greatest risk for such injuries, but even if their feet are wet throughout the day they can be dried and warmed at night. Simple awareness of the potential for injury by prolonged wetness in a cold climate should prompt adequate protective measures.

DIAGNOSIS

The earliest symptoms of trench foot among the British soldiers in the Falklands were variable. For some the first evidence of this disorder was numbness, which generally appeared after seven to ten days. Others had paresthesias (prickling or tingling sensations, or feelings like electric shocks) that made sleep difficult. For some, pain was the initial symptom and also caused problems with sleep. Pain that was almost unbearable upon first putting weight on the feet in the morning was typical. The symptoms tended to spread slowly upward along the leg.

The earliest visible sign of injury is redness of the skin (Figure H in color insert). With greater damage the tissues become swollen. In the Falklands, feet were commonly so swollen that soldiers had difficulty putting on their boots in the morning. With more severe injuries the feet become quite red, greater swelling is present, and large blisters develop. Such changes are usually associated with severe sensory abnormalities. Rarely, the feet become obviously dead or gangrenous, which happened to soldiers who wore their boots for days to weeks without taking them off (Figure I in color insert).

A combination of two classifications of the severity of trench foot developed during World War II is listed below.

FEATURES OF TRENCH FOOT OF DIFFERENT SEVERITY

GRADE	CHARACTERISTIC	FEATURES
Minimal	Reddening of the skin	Slight sensory change
Mild	Swelling	Sensory changes (reversible)
Moderate	Swelling, redness, blebs, and intracutaneous hemorrhage	Irreversible nerve damage
Severe	Severe swelling, blebs, massive bleeding into the skin and other tissues	Gangrene

A cold recovery test can be conducted to determine the long-term circulatory deficit resulting from nonfreezing cold injury. A twenty-four-hour life raft survival exercise was conducted with eleven university students in an indoor pool. The exercise included a six-hour period in which rain was simulated by spraying tap water (temperature approximately 46° F [8° C]) on the raft with a sprinkler. The raft floor was covered with water for most of this period. A few days after the simulation, six of the students reported symptoms that included reddening of the skin, swelling, pain, and tingling. Ruling out other causes, such as chemicals in the water or irritation by the raft material, led to the conclusion the students had the initial stages of nonfreezing cold injury—immersion foot.

A cold-stress recovery test was conducted a few weeks after the simulation. Following a one-minute foot exposure to 59° F (15° C) water, an unaffected student quickly recovered normal toe temperatures. However, a symptomatic student had precooling toe temperatures 5° to 12° F (3° to 7° C) lower than normal and a very slow recovery to temperatures about 18° F (10° C) below normal. This experience provided valuable insight into how short a period of cold stress can cause nonfreezing cold injury and that sequelae include compromised vascular recovery from cold, a phenomenon that could render an individual more susceptible to subsequent cold injury. However, all of the students were symptom free several months later.

TREATMENT

Little definitive treatment of trench foot is possible; usually little is necessary. The most widely used measures consist of keeping the feet clean and dry and keeping them elevated to help relieve the swelling. The person must be kept warm so the feet can have a generous blood supply.

For more severe injuries, debridement, resection of portions of the foot, or even amputation may be necessary, but such treatment must be carried out in a hospital setting and individual needs vary widely.

PROGNOSIS

Almost no one recovers completely from trench foot. Most affected individuals have a permanent reduced tolerance for cold. Most of the British soldiers in the Falklands appeared to have recovered by the time their troopships returned to Great Britain, or by three and one-half months after the end of the fighting. However, randomly selected soldiers were found to have damaged nerves (demyelinated medial or lateral plantar nerves). Many had residual cold sensitivity evidenced by marked vascular constriction in response to only moderate cold stimuli, and a tendency for the constriction to persist in spite of rewarming. Whether troops injured by cold can be effective again in a cold environment appears doubtful.

Individuals with trench foot severe enough to require surgery would be too disabled to continue their military careers. A few individuals have required amputation for intractable pain resulting from nerve damage months or years after the initial injury.

WARM WATER IMMERSION FOOT AND PADDY FOOT

Soldiers in Vietnam and other campaigns have developed injuries from prolonged, intermittent immersion of their feet in warm water. With warm water immersion foot, the wrinkling of the soles of the feet typical of water immersion for a few minutes is greatly exaggerated when the feet are exposed to intermittent wetness for three to ten days. As a result, the soles of the feet become swollen and painful, particularly over the weight-bearing areas on the heels and balls of the foot.

This type of injury, although not a cold injury, is similar to trench foot. Injury is probably produced by trauma to the skin on the sole of a foot that has already been softened, and perhaps damaged, by prolonged wetness.

Paddy foot, an injury which can extend to the tops of the feet and the lower legs, results from almost continuous—rather than intermittent—wetness of the feet for forty-eight to sixty hours. The first symptom is itching, which is followed by the appearance of numerous small blisters, redness, bleeding into the skin, a dull aching with walking, and swelling of the foot that is hard (nonpitting edema). Most victims cannot walk. According to one report, 20 percent of soldiers constantly in water for 72 hours, and 80 percent of those constantly in water for 120 hours, were incapacitated.

Drying the feet and keeping them elevated is the only treatment needed. Most individuals with this condition have been able to return to duty in forty-eight hours to two weeks.

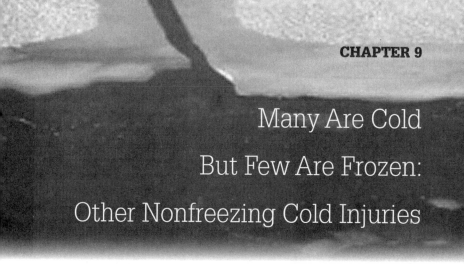

CHAPTER 9

Many Are Cold But Few Are Frozen: Other Nonfreezing Cold Injuries

A NUMBER OF ADDITIONAL INJURIES can be produced by cold. Most are primarily nuisances, but cold-induced urticaria can be lethal, and others can be annoying and to some extent disabling.

CHILBLAINS AND PERNIO

Chilblains and pernio are nonfreezing cold injuries first described by Corlett in 1894. They are sometimes referred to as a single entity, but differences exist. Unlike frostbite, which results from exposure to freezing temperatures, these disorders occur in moderately cold, damp climates such as northern Europe, the northeastern United States, or maritime Canada. A genetic factor has been implicated.

Chilblains are localized abnormalities (lesions) that occur after exposure to nonfreezing cold and wet environments. They usually are swollen and tender, have a reddish purple color, and itch. Sometimes blisters develop. The skin may be somewhat blue. Flaking and scaling may occur but deep tissue damage, as seen with frostbite or trench foot, does not develop. Lesions may be found on the hands, ears, lower legs, and feet. Water sports such as rafting, kayaking, and canoeing predispose to this type of injury. Sensitivity to pressure caused by footwear is a common complaint.

Pernio occurs after twelve hours to three days of exposure to cold, wet environments and consists of painful blisters that may form dark crusts and eventually slough. Typically, these lesions appear on the thighs. They are frequent among female equestrians wearing jodhpurs. Persistent tingling or buzzing sensations (paresthesias) are not uncommon. The lesions are self-limited and resolve over one to three weeks after the instigating conditions are removed.

In normal individuals exposed to cold, cutaneous blood vessels constrict, and subsequently dilate in attempts to maintain perfusion. Individuals who develop chilblains have persistent dilation of small superficial vessels and persistent constriction of larger arterioles.

Individuals with underlying vascular abnormalities such as Raynaud's disease, arteriosclerosis, anorexia, or some other disorders may have lesions that last for months or recur.

Patchy osteoporosis and small bone defects have been described in children. These bone defects occur as a result of vascular constriction, and subsequent bone death (infarction). No treatment is required and the bones return to normal over time.

Prevention and Treatment

Both chilblains and pernio should be prevented. Warm clothing and warm housing dramatically reduce the incidence of these disorders. Good foot hygiene, keeping the feet dry, and massaging them to stimulate blood flow also help.

Treatment modalities for chilblains are broad. Topical corticosteroids such as hydrocortisone and calcium channel blockers such as nifedipine, ketorolac, nicotinic acid, and topical minoxidil (all of which require a physician's prescription) have been used.

COLD PANNICULITIS IN CHILDREN

Many types of panniculitis (inflammation of the fat beneath the skin) affect all age groups. Cold panniculitis is a syndrome resulting from cold exposure that has a predilection for infants and small children. It is characterized by the appearance of warm, nontender, red to purple, firm subcutaneous plaques, typically on the cheeks and forehead. The lesions appear six to eight hours after exposure to cold air or cold objects such as popsicles, ice, or teething rings. The lesions last for two to six weeks and resolve without treatment. Cold panniculitis does not produce significant secondary consequences, although isolated instances of residual hyperpigmentation have been reported. Unlike other cold-induced skin changes such as trench foot, or frostbite, which may affect the skin and subcutaneous tissues, cold panniculitis only affects the subcutaneous fatty layer and has a much better prognosis.

The earliest report of cold panniculitis was in 1902 by Hochsiger, who described tenderness, redness, and hardening in the skin beneath the lower jaw of children exposed to cold.

The propensity for cold panniculitis to occur in infants and children results from the higher content of saturated fatty acids in the subcutaneous layer. The ratio of saturated fatty acid (palmitic acid—melting point 63.1° C) to unsaturated fatty acid (oleic acid—melting point 13.4° C) is three times higher in infants than adults. (Adult levels of unsaturation are reached by the first few months of life.) Saturated fatty acids solidify at a higher ambient temperature. In one study, investigators suggested dietary differences in infants might influence the composition of subcutaneous fat, thereby contributing to susceptibility to cold panniculitis.

Ice has been implicated in the development of this disorder. Applying ice to the inner aspect of the forearm induces cold panniculitis in all newborns, 40 percent of six-month-olds, and rarely after nine months of age. These lesions develop in fifteen minutes to forty-eight hours.

Numerous studies detail the benign nature of cold panniculitis. The paucity of reports of cold panniculitis in the medical literature appears to have no correlation with the frequency with which it is encountered in general pediatric practice and emergency departments.

In view of the benign nature of cold panniculitis, observation and reassurance for the parents is all that is needed.

COLD-INDUCED URTICARIA

Urticaria, or hives, a vascular reaction of the skin and other tissues characterized by the eruption of pale evanescent wheals, is a common disorder affecting up to 20 percent of the population. The spectrum of clinical presentations is broad, ranging from insignificant skin lesions to shock and even death.

Urticaria may be acute (less than six weeks duration) or chronic (greater than six weeks duration). Acute urticaria is most frequently seen in individuals prone to develop allergies. In contrast, chronic urticaria is less common and is often a diagnostic dilemma.

A study of ninety-four children with chronic urticaria found that 84 percent had undetermined etiologies. Cold urticaria accounted for one of the remaining 16 percent. Despite its rare occurrence, failure to recognize the disorder may result in unnecessary disability or even death.

Exposure to cold may result in the development of scattered or generalized urticaria within minutes, or a shock-like state with a potentially fatal outcome. The type of cold exposure may result in a predictive symptom complex. Consumption of cold foods may result in localized swelling (angioedema) of the lips, oral tissues, and throat, whereas cold water aquatic events may induce systemic symptoms that are analogous to anaphylactic shock and include fainting, dizziness, low blood pressure, abdominal pain, and confusion or disorientation.

The diagnosis of cold urticaria is often determined by a cold stimulation test during which an ice cube is placed on the forearm for twenty minutes. A positive result consists of the development of a wheal. This test is often used to delineate the types of cold urticaria.

TYPES OF URTICARIA

FAMILIAL COLD URTICARIA
- o Inherited as an autosomal dominant.
- o Presents in the first week of life after exposure to a cold, damp, or windy environment.
- o Children present with delayed urticaria thirty minutes to three hours after exposure.
- o Fever, chills, and edema of the hands and feet are often present.
- o Ice cube test is negative.

ACQUIRED COLD URTICARIA
- o May be of unknown origin with no preceding disease or infection.
- o Symptoms may be scattered or localized urticaria, or life-threatening anaphylaxis.

In a study of thirty-five children and adults, the development of localized angioedema following consumption of ice-cold foods was found to be a good clinical predictor of those who would develop a shock-like state upon exposure to cold water. Based on this data, a classification system was designed to aid physicians in recommending aquatic activities for those patients with a history of cold water-induced urticaria.

- o Group 1: Localized urticaria
- o Group 2: Generalized urticaria without angioedema of the mouth and throat
- o Group 3: Angioedema of the mouth and throat

Individuals who present with no or few urticaria after cold water exposure may be pretreated with an antihistamine or slow and gradual exposure to cold water. Avoidance of cold water activities is recommended for those persons in group three whose symptoms occur after the ingestion of cold food.

BREATHING IN THE COLD

Although humans poorly tolerate cold stress to the noninsulated body surface, very cold air can be breathed by healthy individuals with little thermal consequence. However, asthma induced by exercise or cold is a commonly recognized respiratory disorder.

Asthma is characterized by constriction of the smaller air passages (bronchioles) and by increased production of mucus by the membranes lining these structures, both of which impair the passage of air. In most individuals an allergic reaction is responsible for the development of asthma, but in some persons exercise or exposure to cold can set it off.

In these individuals the disorder may be mediated by the direct effect of airway cooling or drying, neural sensory receptors and airway reflexes, or release of various unidentified chemical mediators. Airway drying alone, with the subsequent concentration of airway lining fluid has been proposed as the major stimulus for airway narrowing. However, mounting evidence supports the additional, but not exclusive, influence of airway cooling itself.

Cold exposure may also affect the pulmonary circulation. Cold appears to potentiate the effects of hypoxia on the pulmonary circulation and to contribute to high-altitude illnesses, which may explain the higher incidence of acute mountain sickness and high-altitude pulmonary edema in climbers during seasons of colder ambient temperatures and at similar high altitudes in northern as opposed to tropical areas.

Acute Clinical Disorders

The incidence of reactions to exercise in cold air is similar in children and adults. About 70 to 80 percent of asthmatics and 3 to 10 percent of otherwise asymptomatic athletes experience exercise-induced asthma. Breathing cold air and exercise are separate stimuli for bronchiole constriction that may act synergistically.

Usually few symptoms occur during the period of exercise or at the time of rapid breathing of cold, dry air. The effects become maximal within five to fifteen minutes after the stimulus—the early phase response. Spontaneous recovery usually takes place within thirty minutes to two hours, and usually is followed by a refractory period of one to two hours during which responses to further stimuli are attenuated. A late-phase response may occur four to ten hours after the stimulus.

Reasons for the delay in the onset of symptoms are unknown. However, since catecholamines (such as adrenaline) and other β agonists relax airway smooth muscle, the normal increase in plasma catecholamine levels during exercise may provide protection during and immediately after exercise until catecholamine levels return to baseline levels. The severity of the early phase symptoms is dependent on the thermal load placed on the airways—the speed and depth of breathing, the temperature and water content of the inspired air, and the length of exposure.

Airway obstruction declines in response to repetitive bouts of exercise within one to two hours of the initial bout. Although the mechanisms are not clear, one explanation for this refractory period is depletion of histamine and other mediators during the early response.

The existence of an exercise-related late phase response is controversial. However, in some individuals airway resistance increases again four to ten hours after stimulus. This reaction does not occur in all affected individuals. Some data indicate an acclimatization effect: physically fit asthmatics have less exercise-induced asthma than those who are untrained. In many individuals, symptoms are greater in early winter than in late winter.

The standard and most effective method of pharmacologic prevention is inhaling a β agonist fifteen to thirty minutes prior to exposures that the person knows from experience trigger attacks. The bronchial changes that usually lead to an attack are not prevented, but the final step, smooth muscle contraction that narrows the bronchioles, is attenuated by the direct action of the β agonist. Other agents may be added. In some subjects only administering medication prior to exposure is not sufficient. For such individuals the routine use of inhaled corticosteroids and other drugs effectively reduce the inflammation usually present.

Nonpharmacologic approaches are also useful and often reduce the need for medication. A fifteen to twenty minute warm-up of submaximal exercise prior to vigorous exercise is often protective. Using face masks to rebreathe some of the humidified, warm, expired air, a high level of physical conditioning, and avoiding exercise in contaminated environments are recommended.

Some cold-sensitive individuals cough following hyperventilation or exercise in moderately cold air. Maximum cough frequency occurs within five minutes of terminating the activity, and may be another symptom of asthma induced by exercise or cold. Cross-country skiers who train heavily or race at temperatures below -4° F (-20° C) have a high incidence of dry cough lasting from days to a week. High breathing rates in very cold air can also cause enough damage by nasal mucosal drying to lead to nose bleeds.

Exercise or heavy work in very cold air can cause a burning sensation in the chest that is often described as freezing of the lungs. Frosting of the lungs in horses in extreme arctic conditions as well as sled dogs dying from collection of fluid in the lung under these conditions have been reported. Arctic hunters also have reported freezing of the lungs under heavy work loads in severely cold air. These reports are anecdotal, however, and the extent to which lung tissue is actually cooled or damaged is not known. Cold air (-58° to -18° F or -50° to -28° C) delivered to the larynx of anesthetized dogs for 20 to 133 minutes produced no freezing injury to any respiratory tissue. Temperature of the inspired air rose to at least 68° F (20° C) at the origin of the bronchi. Although no freezing injury occurred, obstruction by severe upper airway swelling was produced if the cooling was severe enough.

An aviator exposed to air temperatures of -58° F (-50°C) at speeds of up to 157 mph (258 km/h) sustained severe frostbite of the face and fingers, but no evidence of freezing injury to the bronchi or lungs could be found. He did, however, experience obstructive swelling in the mouth, nose, and pharynx that required insertion of a breathing tube in his throat (tracheostomy). After recovery, he had no additional pulmonary complications.

Chronic Clinical Disorders

Several reports have linked cold weather to an increased incidence of upper airway infections. In Norway, the frequency of sinusitis is greater in northern than in southern communities and is greater in autumn than in spring. The infection rate could increase due to more crowded living conditions, or a greater amount of time spent indoors during cold weather months.

Epidemiological studies have disclosed a condition in older male Eskimos labeled "Eskimo lung." These men have symptoms similar to chronic obstructive pulmonary disease (COPD, or emphysema): decreased air flow rates, cough, wheezing, large lung volume, and increased pulmonary artery diameter. The symptoms of Eskimo lung have been related to hard work in severely cold winters. Younger inhabitants of Arctic Bay, who have not followed old hunting traditions and the more modernized Inuvik do not have such a high prevalence of COPD. Eskimo lung may be related to other conditions such as smoking, but no data correlate a higher smoking rate in the northern populations with the greater incidence of COPD.

Until recently tuberculosis was prevalent in northern communities. Although some correlation has been found with cold conditions, crowded living conditions and poor nutrition appear equally or more responsible for the high incidence of this infection.

COLD-INDUCED VASOMOTOR RHINITIS (RUNNY NOSE)

Cold exposure often elicits vasomotor rhinitis; inflammation of the nasal mucosa that causes a runny nose. This is a common disorder of children and adults who enjoy the outdoors. It is not a serious condition; it is a nuisance.

Some individuals encountering cold air develop a runny nose (rhinorhea) that produces clear, thin mucus associated with congestion. It is caused by an imbalance in the autonomic nerve supply to the nasal mucosa. Cold air stimulation results in the inhibition of the sympathetic vasomotor responses, relaxation of the smooth muscle of the nares, and enhancement of the parasympathetic vasomotor response. Mucous glands are activated by this parasympathetic stimulation through acetylcholine. Anticholinergic drugs can inhibit the receptors of these glands.

Cooling of the feet and dry, cold air stimulation of the nasal mucosa in individuals with allergic rhinitis were compared to those with vasomotor rhinitis and normal controls with a technique for measuring the volume of the nasal cavity. This volume was also measured quickly and comfortably (compared to previous methods) with intranasal balloons.

Individuals had both lower extremities immersed to the level of the ankles into cold water (55° F or 13° C) for approximately five minutes. In the second part of the study, dry, cold air (55° F or 13° C) was passed through the nostrils for five minutes. Following each stimulation, the quantity of nasal secretions and nasal volume were measured at specified intervals.

Individuals with vasomotor rhinitis had a greater decrease in nasal volume and a greater volume of nasal secretions than those with allergic rhinitis and the control group after five minutes of immersion of the feet. Dry, cold air inhalation initially caused the largest reduction in nasal volume in individuals with vasomotor rhinitis, but all groups had nasal volume reduction after fifteen minutes.

Ipratropium bromide (IBNS), an anticholinergic agent available as a nasal spray, has been shown to be effective in the treatment of cold-induced rhinitis.

RAYNAUD'S PHENOMENON

Raynaud's phenomenon occurs in about 5 percent of the population, is about four times more common in women, and is basically an overreaction to cold exposure. The body's initial response to cold is vasoconstriction in the skin, which shunts blood away from the surface, causing the surface tissues to become pale and lose sensation. It occurs most commonly in the fingers, toes, ears, and nose. Once the condition has developed, it recurs whenever the affected parts are exposed to cool temperatures, such as swimming in 60° to 70° F (15° to 21° C) water.

Raynaud's is characterized by both extreme vasoconstriction and failed vasodilation. The initial vasoconstriction is profound, resulting in blanched skin. During rewarming the vasodilation that should follow the initial vasoconstriction to maintain circulation does not occur. The problem appears to lie in the sympathetic innervation of the arteriovenous anastomoses, where shunting of blood between the arterial and venous circulations normally occurs.

Decreased circulation resulting from this vasoconstriction causes the change in skin color and the loss of sensation. It also increases the risk of frostbite in the affected digits. When the affected area is rewarmed, the vasculature opens widely, reestablishing circulation, and causing the skin to become red. Throbbing pain that typically lasts five to ten minutes, and occasionally itching, may develop.

Each time this cycle of cold-vasoconstriction to warm-vasodilatation takes place, the vasoconstriction tends to occur with less stimulation, and the rewarming symptoms tend to be worse and more painful. Raynaud's tends to worsen with age.

Management

○ A correct diagnosis must be made. Is the condition primary Raynaud's caused by cold exposure, or is it secondary Raynaud's symptomatic of another disease?

○ Cold exposure should be avoided or limited, and the affected area should be effectively insulated and kept dry.

○ Medications that can make Raynaud's worse should be avoided.

○ Nicotine, caffeine, alcohol, and over-the-counter decongestants should be avoided.

○ Calcium channel blockers are considered the most effective pharmacological treatment. Nifedipine XL, 30 to 90 mg orally once a day, is the drug of choice. If it is not effective, or if side effects occur, another calcium channel blocker, such as diltiazem, 30 to 120 mg orally once a day, or felodipine, 2.5 to 10 mg orally once a day, can be tried. Verapamil has not been found to be effective.

Pavlovian Response Treatment

Pavlovian responses can be used to treat Raynaud's. This noninvasive, non-pharmacological technique attempts to change the neurovascular response to cold exposure. Blood vessels can be trained to dilate rather than constrict when exposed to cold.

Insulated containers such as drink coolers are needed, the number depending upon the number of hands or feet being treated. Warm water and a cool environment are also necessary. The goal is to cool the head and trunk while keeping the hands and feet warm.

The containers should be filled with warm water—105° to 110° F (40° to 43° C). One should be placed inside where it is warm, and another placed outside or in a site where it is cold. The persons should dress for comfort in the warm site, not the cool one, as they need to cool slightly while in the cool spot.

Individuals should start in the warm site and sit with feet or hands in the warm water (105°–110° F [40°–43° C]) for two to five minutes. Then they should wrap their hands or feet in a towel to keep them warm, go to the cool site and do the same: sit, allowing the head and body to sense the cold air, and place the extremities in the warm water for about ten minutes. This process should then be repeated.

The technique works best if three to six trials are carried out per day: warm air for two to five minutes, cold air for ten minutes, then warm air and cold air again every other day for a total of fifty trials (eight to sixteen days). The procedure is inexpensive and quite safe. Responses vary. Often it helps, but if it does not, nothing has been lost but a little time.

IS RAYNAUD'S PRIMARY OR SECONDARY?

Raynaud's phenomenon is considered primary when no cause can be found. Raynaud's that is caused by another illness is considered secondary. Anyone with Raynaud's symptoms should see a physician, as they may be an indication of underlying disease.

Raynaud's phenomenon may be a symptom of:

- CREST syndrome
- Scleroderma
- Mixed connective tissue diseases, polymyositis, dermatomyositis
- Systemic lupus erythematosus
- Rheumatoid arthritis
- Buerger's disease
- Polycythemia, cryoglobulinemia
- Carpal tunnel syndrome
- Estrogen replacement therapy without progesterone
- Drug therapy with beta blockers, ergotamine, methysergide, vinblastine, beleomycin, or oral contraceptives

CHAPTER 10

I Have Nothing to Wear:
Cold Weather Clothing

THE FOUR INNS WALK, an annual competitive hike over the English moors, is forty-five miles (seventy-three kilometers) long, with a total ascent of about 4,500 feet (1,400 m). In 1964 this competition was held in weather that proved disastrous. A heavy rain was falling. Winds as strong as 29 mph (47 km/h) were measured at sea level. Even stronger winds were probably encountered on the moors. Temperatures ranged from 32° to 45° F (0° to 7° C).

Two hundred and forty hikers attempted the course. Usually two-thirds of the competitors finish, but in this year only twenty-two finished. Three hikers died of hypothermia. Four others were rescued in critical condition. Although the hikers were exercising at a very high work rate and were producing large amounts of metabolic heat, they were inadequately clothed. Many were wearing only shorts and a tee shirt.

This event clearly demonstrated that humans cannot compensate for severe cold with heat generated by exercise alone; in adverse environments, effective clothing is required to prevent excessive heat loss. In fact, in harsher conditions, such as a blizzard, clothing alone may not provide adequate protection, and some type of shelter may also be necessary. This chapter focuses on the principles of clothing material, design, and use.

Three principles should be followed in choosing cold-weather clothing. First, clothing must be selected as a complete ensemble that is designed for the specific conditions the wearer expects to encounter. This includes not only environmental conditions—temperature, humidity, rain or snow, wind—but also the type of physical activity to be performed—continuous or intermittent, prolonged or brief, low or high intensity.

Second, the principles of how clothing works must be understood, and clothing must be maintained and used properly, which can widen the window of conditions in which a specific clothing ensemble can be used.

Third, and most important, moisture accumulation in clothing must be minimized. Cold weather enthusiasts must rigorously do everything possible to keep water out of their clothing (Figure 10-1).

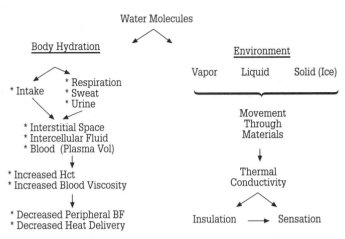

Figure 10-1. Fate of water molecules. Although water is vital for hydration and body function, water greatly decreases clothing insulation and personal comfort.

SPECIFIC CONSIDERATIONS

The materials used in cold weather clothing must fulfill four important functions—insulation, moisture transfer, water resistance, and wind resistance.

○ *Insulation*—The insulating value of clothing material is primarily dependent on its thickness; its ability to trap air, which acts as an insulator; and its moisture content.

○ *Moisture Transfer*—Moisture is produced at the skin through sweating, most of which is insensible in cold climates. As much water as possible must pass from the skin through the clothing, either in vapor or liquid form. Permeable fabrics allow vaporized moisture to pass through them. Liquid transfer occurs when perspiration can pass along the fibers to the clothing surface where it evaporates. Moisture that remains within the material results in conductive heat loss that can decrease thermal insulation by as much as 30 to 50 percent.

○ *Water Resistance*—Clothing materials that repel liquid minimize entry of water into the material, which helps maintain the insulation value and the comfort of the garment.

○ *Wind Resistance*—A material's resistance to airflow (wind) is very significant because moving air carries heat away from the skin surface (convection).

Another characteristic of clothing material that is important because it may have adverse effects is how likely the material is to retain water. Water can be held within material by three different mechanisms (Figure 10-2).

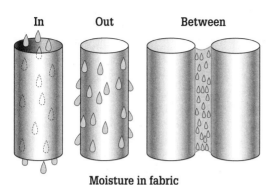

In   Out   Between

Moisture in fabric

Figure 10-2. Water can accumulate in fabric by being absorbed inside the fibers, absorbed along the outside of fibers, and by capillary action between parallel fibers and surfaces.

Generally, most water is held by capillary action—through surface tension—between parallel fibers or material surfaces and is removed by spinning or wringing out the material. The next most prevalent source of water in wet clothing is water absorbed within the fibers, which must be removed by evaporation. The table on page 104 compares fiber absorption for several common materials. Finally, some water is adsorbed on the outside surface of material fibers.

Unless wet clothing is spun or wrung out, the major avenue for drying is evaporation. It takes 580 calories of energy to evaporate one gram of liquid water, and while this energy can be drawn from the environment, this process is very slow. The human body provides a quicker source of heat but the energy demands are enormous. If a garment is soaked with one liter of water, evaporating that 1,000 grams of water would require 580 kilocalories, which is approximately one-fourth of the total dietary caloric intake for one day for an average individual. Clearly, water retention must be considered when choosing an ensemble.

Comfort affects the wearer's perception of clothing effectiveness. Fit is important. If multiple layers are included in an ensemble, each layer must be large enough to fit loosely over the one beneath.

GENERAL GUIDELINES FOR CHOOSING CLOTHING

Collars—Garments should have high collars that zip up to the top edge, providing a high turtleneck. Such collars increase comfort because the neck is particularly sensitive to cold air currents. The high collar can also provide frostbite protection to the lower face.

Hoods—An insulated hood is essential for cold weather. (Insulation may be increased by adding a close-fitting cap underneath a hood.) Although the amount of heat lost through the head is greatly overemphasized, a good hood does minimize such loss, blocks uncomfortable cold air currents through the neck of the jacket, and protects the face and ears from frostbite.

Sleeve Ends and Cuffs—Elastic cuffs that close around the wrist help reduce convective cooling of the arms. The interface between mittens and the sleeve end itself also is significant. Unless the mitten fits easily and fully inside or over the sleeve end, bunching of the mitten against the sleeve creates a weakness in the insulating armor. Cold wrists are common with poorly integrated jacket-mitten combinations.

Pockets—Pockets in an outer jacket should be large enough to carry everything needed (including mittens), should be easy to open with mittens on, and must close easily and securely to prevent loss of contents. Openings should be as close to horizontal as possible to maximize the volume of material that can be put in the pocket and minimize the possibility of contents falling out. Unfortunately, style often takes priority over function when clothing is designed, and pockets are small with openings that are slanted or even vertical.

Zippers—Zippers must be operable with mittens on, which can be greatly facilitated by attaching two- to three-inch (five- to eight-centimeter) tabs to each zipper. Fashion may dictate that zippers be small and inconspicuous, but small zippers catch or snag more often and are more prone to break. They are also considerably more difficult to operate, even with tabs.

Length and Coverage—A common weakness in clothing ensembles is inadequate thermal insulation at the waist. Upper and lower body garments should either be continuous or overlapping. Fashionable short jackets should be foregone for longer models that overlap the pants and protect the seat while sitting. Extra protection can also be gained by switching from pants to a bib design for the outer layer.

Ventilation—A clothing ensemble must be capable of being ventilated while in use. Clothing ventilation removes water vapor from inside the ensemble and allows convective, conductive, evaporative, and even radiative heat loss from the skin surface. Ventilation may be facilitated by open sleeve ends, armpit zippers, and front zippers (a reason not to use a pullover design). The armpit zippers should be long enough to allow arms to be inserted through them, if increased radiative and convective heat loss from the arms is needed.

Rainwear—Certain elements of design are essential for rainwear to be effective. The hood must close snugly enough to keep water out but should not restrict movement of the head. The hood also must be large enough to fit over whatever headgear is being worn. Shoulder seams leak notoriously. Preferably, no seams should extend across the top of the shoulders where they can be distorted by pack straps. Dropped seams that run across the front or back of the shoulder area or raglan sleeves that extend in one piece to the neckline are more suitable. Special care must be taken with the seams regardless of where they are located. The number of seams should be minimized, and they must be sealed.

CHOOSING CLOTHING MATERIALS

No third-party testing facility, such as the Underwriters' Laboratory, exists for clothing. Consumers are at the mercy of advertising agents serving the manufacturers and merchants. The most reliable indicator of a fabric's or garment's performance is its persistence in the market place for two to three years or more.

A variety of natural materials are used in clothing for outdoor wear. Wool, cotton, silk, and goose down are the most popular. All but down are usually combined with synthetic materials such as nylon, polypropylene, polyester, and acrylics to impart specific desirable characteristics to the fabric. Materials should be chosen according to how they function in the total clothing ensemble.

Underwear

Underclothing must maintain a dry layer of insulation immediately adjacent to the skin. Because underwear can be moistened by perspiration it must promote moisture passage along the material fibers (commonly referred to as wicking), should absorb little water within its fibers, and should retain its insulating ability when wet.

Polypropylene became popular for underwear in the 1970s. Because it is hydrophobic (tends to repel, not absorb, water) and allows moisture to wick along the fibers—from the skin surface to the surface of the fabric where it evaporates—it provides a greater sensation of warmth. Furthermore, polypropylene retains most of its insulating properties when wet. The disadvantages of polypropylene include its retention of body odors—it can become quite foul after repeated use—its tendencies to become brittle when heated and to pill when dried in a clothes dryer, as well as its tendency to become baggy. The last problem has been corrected to a considerable extent by adding nylon to the fabric.

Polyester fabrics have to a large extent replaced polypropylene because, in spite of being slightly more expensive, they do not have the same disadvantages. Capilene, Coolmax, Thermax, and Thermostat are some of the trademarks of polyester fabrics.

These fabrics keep the skin cool and dry through a wide range of activity, but to achieve this effect they must be worn next to the skin, not over cotton underwear or as a jacket.

Although widely used, cotton is a poor fabric for underwear worn in outdoor situations, primarily because cotton fibers absorb so much water (up to 40 percent of the material's weight in water). Also, wet cotton loses essentially all of its insulation value, is heavy, and is very slow to dry. In a wilderness context, cotton is often referred to as the "death fiber."

AMOUNT OF WATER THAT CAN BE ABSORBED WITHIN DIFFERENT FABRICS AS A PERCENTAGE OF WEIGHT.

FABRIC	AFTER SOAKING
Cotton	40%
Silk	36%
Wool	34%
Nylon	10%
Polyester	0.9%
Polypropylene	0.2%

Wool is an excellent fabric for underwear, but until newer varieties came on the market, wool was often avoided because it has large fibers that are itchy and slow to dry. Adding a small amount (one tablespoon) of olive oil to the wash water can eliminate the scratchiness that older wool tends to develop after repeating washings. Marino wool from Australia has recently become popular because it has thinner, softer fibers that are much more comfortable against the skin. Wool fibers are resilient, strong, and provide loft—the fibers trap air between them, thus providing insulation. The core of the wool fiber is hydrophilic. As water vapor is produced by the skin, it is taken up by the core of the fiber. Wool can carry up to 30 percent of its dry weight in water without feeling wet.

Even though wool absorbs nearly as much water (34 percent of its weight) as cotton (40 percent of its weight), wool has two huge advantages over cotton: the insulation it provides when wet and its ability to dry quickly. Wet cotton fibers mat together so no air is trapped between them to provide insulation. Also water can only evaporate from the inside and outside surfaces of a cotton garment. Wool, on the other hand, is resilient and traps air between the wet fibers. As a result a wet wool garment retains much of its insulation. Wool fibers also dry faster because there is much more surface area from which water can evaporate. Evaporation occurs not only from the material surfaces but also from the surface of each individual fiber. Newer Marino wool dries even faster because the fibers have a smaller diameter. Each fiber holds less water and has a much greater relative surface area from which water can evaporate.

One of the writers recently wore Marino wool underwear on a twenty-six-day winter expedition. The clothing was comfortable, durable, warm, generally stayed dry, and was easy to dry if it did become wet. It did not retain body odor even after continuous wear, day and night, for almost a month.

Some people like the feel of silk. However, silk holds 36 percent of its weight in water and feels unpleasant when it becomes wet.

Insulating Layers

Wool has long been popular for caps and gloves and is becoming more popular for upper- and lower-body clothing. Its major disadvantage is its greater weight and lower resistance to abrasion than pile or fleece, by which it has been replaced to a considerable extent. It is also expensive. However, Marino wool has many properties that make it more comfortable, allow it to maintain insulation when wet, and to dry more quickly.

Synthetic fabrics are very popular. Pile fabrics, introduced in the 1970s, are lighter and are hydrophobic. However, they tended to lose their pile and to pill badly with wear and laundering, and have largely been replaced by fleece.

Fleece is a similar polyester fabric, but with stiffer fibers than pile, and superior qualities. It is produced in different thicknesses: microfleece for underwear and in 100, 200, and 300 weights (grams/m^2) for outer garments. This material breathes well and is lightweight, durable, and fast drying. It is easy to cut and sew. When wet, fleece and pile can be wrung almost dry, allowing them to retain most of their insulating value. On the down side, like knitted materials, these fabrics are porous and provide little protection from wind.

Goose down is the best available insulating material for its weight—when it is dry. True down is the philoplume of geese or ducks and historically was handpicked from live animals, but that material is no longer available. Down now comes from killed animals and is composed of less mature plumes that do not loft as well. However, down garments drape well, do not constrict movement, loft after compression, and are comfortable. When wet, down mats together and loses most of its insulating properties. However, when precipitation is in the form of dry snow, which is typical of high altitudes, down is the insulating material of choice.

Synthetic fibers provide insulation and loft similar to down and retain their insulating properties when wet. Also, they are less expensive. Dacron, Hollofill, and Quallofil are trade names for early down replacements (Figure 10-3). The latter two had one and four hollow cores respectively, which trapped dead air within the fibers to increase insulation. Primaloft and Liteloft are more recent materials that use a combination of three different fiber diameters (deniers); they trap air between fibers to increase insulation and provide high loft. The disadvantages of such materials are their greater weight (about 50 percent heavier than down with the same insulating value), bulk, and lack of compressibility.

Mat materials are composed of extruded, densely packed, fine fibers. These small filaments are said to immobilize as much air as larger filaments in a much thinner layer because the thickness of the layer of air immobilized around the filament is the same regardless of the filament diameter. These garments are not as bulky as those made of larger filaments or down, which appeals to individuals concerned about their appearance. Because the fibers are so thin (five microns in diameter instead of the forty microns typical of

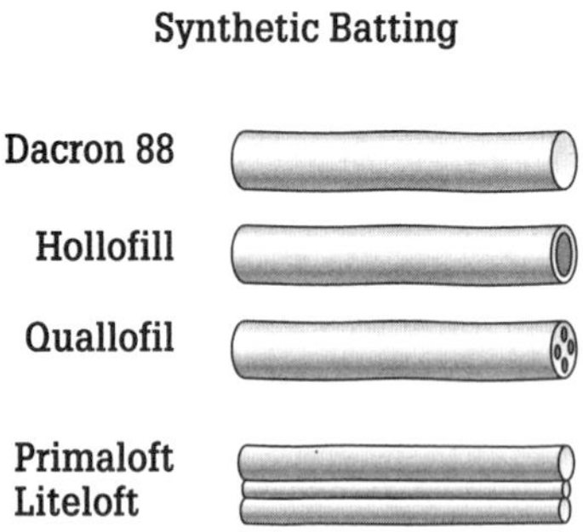

Synthetic Batting

Dacron 88

Hollofill

Quallofil

Primaloft
Liteloft

Figure 10-3. Different types of synthetic fibers that provide loft in a manner similar to down. Hollofill and Quallofil trap air within fibers to create insulation. Primaloft and Liteloft fuse three different diameter fibers together, allowing air to be trapped between fibers, with the larger diameter, stiffer fibers providing the loft.

other synthetic fibers) they slightly limit radiant heat loss, but they lose this advantage when laundered. These materials resist compression and do not conform to the body surface (drape) well, which allows air to circulate beneath the garment, increasing heat loss. Manufacturers use wrist elastic or snaps, waist skirts, and snug necks to reduce this airflow. Also these materials are almost twice as heavy and much less compressible than down of equal insulation value. Thinsulate is the dominant brand of this type of fabric, the use of which is limited largely to ski clothing.

Outer Shell

The outer shell must be windproof, or at least wind resistant, and must repel water in order to protect the insulating qualities of the underlying clothing.

The ideal fabric that would allow all water vapor to pass through freely but keep out all liquid water has yet to be developed. The best available waterproof-breathable fabrics are laminates, which are made up of multiple layers of material, one of which contains numerous minute pores that are large enough to allow water vapor to escape but too small to allow the larger droplets of liquid water to pass through. The best known of these laminates is Gore-Tex, which has a Teflon film applied to the fabric. However, laminates still present some problems. They are expensive, and soiling limits their functionality. The earlier laminates had a tendency to delaminate and could be "poisoned" by perspiration and other substances so they were no longer permeable. Considerable difficulty has been encountered in sealing the seams. Additional problems with laminates include low resistance to abrasion, stiffness, and noisiness.

During heavy exertion, the amount of moisture produced can exceed the capability of a laminate to transmit water vapor. Vents have been placed in some garments made of laminates so that more moisture can escape.

A second type of rainwear fabric is either very tightly woven so that the pores between the threads are very small or is made of two fibers, one of which is cotton, which swells when wet and tends to close off the pores. None of these fabrics provide protection in a heavy rain. Most provide protection from the wind. Water repellent sprays have been used to try to increase (or restore) water repellent qualities.

Some manufacturers have resorted to completely waterproof materials or coatings and have tried to design openings that would allow perspiration to evaporate. One such garment that has been around for many years is the poncho, which can be worn loosely so that water vapor escapes below its skirt. However, with heavy exertion perspiration still soaks the wearer.

Another lesson learned from the Four Inns tragedy was the need to protect the lower extremities from wind and water as well as the upper body. The same materials can be used for rain pants as are used for rain jackets.

METALLIZED REFLECTIVE LAYERS

Many claims have been made about the effectiveness of metallized reflective layers (aluminum) for reducing heat loss in the cold. The most common example of this type of product is the so-called space blanket, but the technology is also used in clothing and in thin inner sleeping bags. The theoretical benefit is the ability of the metallized layer to reflect heat radiated from the skin back to the body. The space blanket is often recommended as an efficient warming aid for hypothermia patients.

The effectiveness of reflective layers is limited in two ways. First, radiant heat loss from extremely cold skin is minimal. For a hypothermic individual, the main benefit of a space blanket would be the vapor barrier that would reduce convective and evaporative heat loss.

Second, the reflective layer is most effective if placed on the outside of an uncompressed layer of low density insulation. Radiant heat loss through higher density fibers or foam insulation is minimal, so metallized reflective layers would provide no benefit. In low density, loosely packed materials such as polyester batting, radiant heat loss may be substantial. A reflective layer on the outside of this material would be effective—potentially doubling insulation values—but only if the material is not compressed, in which case radiant heat loss is minimal. Reflective layers in clothing have produced mixed results because movement in clothing causes continued compression of the clothing.

A metallized reflective material in a light sleeping bag inside a regular sleeping bag, but over a full layer of underwear, has more potential for effectiveness. Most of the insulation system is uncompressed and static, and radiant heat may be reflected back to the sleeping individual. One of the authors tested a metallized reflective bag within a heavy down sleeping bag by sleeping outside the barracks at an arctic military base in Alert, Canada. After a few hours, he had to come back into the barracks . . . because he was too hot! In a subsequent training expedition, a thinner down bag was used and the sleeping bag zipper was never completely closed, even with night time temperatures as low as -40° F (-40° C). The effectiveness of any system that includes metallized reflective layers should be confirmed on shorter trips before a longer more-exposed expedition is attempted.

PROTECTING HANDS

Cold, painful fingers and toes are common cold weather complaints but also are among the easiest to remedy if the physiologic reactions to cold are kept in mind. When the body is cooled, its first response is to constrict the blood vessels to the extremities to conserve heat. In a cold environment, warming the body increases the blood flow to the hands and feet and keeps them warm. High-quality boots and mittens are essential for protection from snow and ice, but adding another sweater may be more helpful for keeping hands and feet warm and comfortable.

Mittens are much warmer than gloves. Radiant heat is lost from the surface of protective garments, and the larger the surface area the more heat that is lost. Because the fingers are such narrow cylinders, increasing the thickness of gloves by more than one quarter inch (six mm) increases the surface area to such an extent that the increased heat loss eliminates any benefit from the increased insulation. Because mittens do not have such a relatively large surface area, their thickness can be increased to a much greater extent without a concomitant increase in heat loss. Figure 10-4 illustrates this principle. In addition, in mittens less skin is in close contact with the fabric and a thicker layer of insulating air is present.

The basic components of mittens are an outer shell and inner insulating layer(s). A thin layer of wool, nylon, or silk worn next to the skin is useful

Figure 10-4. Comparison of surface area of bare fingers, fingers in gloves, and fingers in mitts

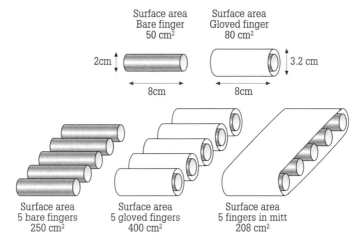

if the mittens have to be removed to manipulate clothing or equipment. The outer shell should be an abrasion-resistant material, typically nylon. Wool works well for insulation, but down and synthetic materials are also used. Large, bulky mittens filled with down or polyester fibers are needed mostly in arctic climates and at very high altitudes—or for individuals who have not learned that the best way to keep the hands and feet warm is to keep the body warm.

PROTECTING FEET

For severely cold climates, particularly for high altitude mountaineering that requires ice climbing, double or triple boots are best. The outer boot is constructed of hard, protective plastic. The inner boot or boots are made of softer insulating material, such as felt or closed cell insulation. The insulating material also covers the bottom of the foot, and the soles are quite thick. Closed cell insulation can increase the risk of frostbite at high altitude as the insulation expands at lower atmospheric pressure, tending to cut off circulation to the feet.

Another type of cold weather boot popular with dog mushers is constructed with a 1.5-inch (3.5 cm) layer of polyurethane foam insulation and covered by Cordura nylon. This boot not only has a thick layer of insulation over the sides and soles, it also breathes.

Older double boots were made of leather, which is entirely adequate, but is heavier than plastic. Leather can be hard enough to protect the feet and soft enough to be flexible. It is porous and breathes, allowing perspiration to evaporate. (For waterproofing, a material should be used that does not block these pores.) Leather can expand to accommodate swelling of feet and ankles due to an upright position or altitude. It remains the best material for single boots in moderately cold climates.

Socks are largely a matter of personal choice. Many experienced hikers prefer an inner thin sock of polyester, silk, nylon, or even lightweight wool, and an outer bulky sock. This combination is useful for reducing friction that can cause blisters, but is not much warmer than a single bulky sock. For warmth, some winter outdoor enthusiasts wear vapor impermeable plastic socks between two wool socks, but this creates problems with perspiration just like vapor barrier boots.

Regardless of the combination of socks chosen, the same total thickness should be worn at all times. Adding extra socks because the weather is colder is an excellent way to ensure that boots are too tight, blood circulation is compromised, and the risk of frostbite is increased. Wearing thinner socks leaves the boots loose and tends to cause blisters.

Gaiters and overboots keep snow out of the top of the boot, which helps avoid wetting and cooling the feet. Some gaiters and overboots have a lining of insulating material such as Ensolite or felt, which does help keep the feet warm in severe conditions.

STRATEGIES FOR USING CLOTHING
Layering

Clothing ensembles should have multiple layers instead of one large thick layer so insulation can be varied to accommodate warmer or colder conditions. In addition, layers should provide abundant ventilation so that moisture removal can be optimized. However, these desirable characteristics are worthless unless the layers and ventilation openings are used properly. Each layer should perform specific functions:

Inner Layer—The inner layer should be highly vapor permeable so that moisture is transferred or "wicked" away from the skin to the next layers of clothing. Dry skin greatly increases the comfort level, particularly the feeling of warmth.

Middle Layers—The middle layers are mostly for insulation and can be composed of a variety of materials. This middle zone should be composed of multiple insulating layers rather than one thick layer to allow for fine tuning the insulation to prevent becoming too warm or too cold.

Outer Layer—The outer layer provides wind and moisture protection. Various materials can be used such as Gore-Tex, 60/40 cloth, Cordura, windstopper (PTFE laminate), nylon, and others.

A common vicious cycle consists of getting cold while preparing or waiting to start working in the cold and putting on several insulating layers. When work or travel begins the person eventually (sometimes quickly) gets warm and moisture begins to accumulate in the clothing. The individual is hesitant to stop to adjust the clothing and puts up with being too warm. Finally, a rest stop is made and layers are taken off to allow cooling. However, no work is being done, heat production is lower, the remaining layers are now wet and uncomfortable, and rapid cooling occurs, which can cause significant discomfort. By the time the person is ready to start again, the insulating layers must be put back on in order to get warm. Work or travel is renewed with all of the clothing on and more heating and moisture accumulation occurs. The individual is even colder during the next break when layers are taken off again, and the cycle continues and gradually gets worse.

The best strategy is proactive layer adjustment. Just before starting, individuals should realize that they are going to get warm, and should remove a layer or two. Even though they feel cold initially, they warm up once they are moving or working. When they stop for a break and heat production is lower, they can put on extra layers of insulation. The inside layers are not as moisture-laden and are more comfortable. Just before starting again, the extra layers should be shed in anticipation of increased heat and moisture production.

In the cold, a cool skin surface is preferable, particularly while working.

Sweating is largely determined by skin temperature, and cooler skin results in less sweat production and less moisture accumulation in clothing.

Moisture Removal

The weekend adventurer syndrome, in which many mistakes are not corrected, but are tolerated because people can put up with almost anything for a few days should be avoided. Allowing moisture to remain in clothing because the trip is short is a recipe for unnecessary discomfort. At the end of the day as much moisture as possible should be extracted from the clothing ensemble in order to restore maximum insulation and comfort for the next day's activities.

Considerable time and effort may be required to dry clothing over a stove or fire, but is worthwhile. Over a week or two, the insulating ability of clothing can decrease considerably even when efforts are made to remove moisture each day. Individuals can get very cold if their clothing loses 30 to 50 percent of its insulation value.

Maintenance

Damage or problems with any element of the clothing ensemble must be repaired. Clothing cannot be expected to perform properly if its physical integrity is compromised. Adequate sewing and repair kits, and knowledge of how to use them at home and in the field, are essential. Care for clothing should be according to manufacturer's instructions. For instance, waterproof, breathable garments should be periodically washed in order to remove dirt particles from the pores and to prevent the moisture transfer characteristics from being compromised.

MOISTURE CONDENSATION WITHIN CLOTHING

Water vapor should pass through clothing layers before condensing into liquid form. If condensation does occur, water should pass through the outside layer of the clothing before it freezes. In a cold environment, moisture can freeze and be trapped within the clothing.

The dew point determines if and where water vapor condenses. If air at a certain temperature is completely saturated with water and its temperature decreases, the capacity of the air to hold water vapor is lowered and some of the vapor condenses to form liquid water. This threshold temperature is the dew point and is illustrated in Figure 10-5.

Figures 10-6 and 10-7 illustrate some problems and solutions caused by different clothing combinations in the cold. When a laminate such as Gore-Tex is worn in below-freezing temperatures, and the dew point is reached on the body side of the laminate membrane, vapor condenses and is trapped inside the garment, where it later freezes. If two layers of insulation are worn, the dew point may be reached between layers and liquid and ice crystals accumulate on the inside of the outer layer from which it can later be brushed off.

Figure 10-5. As air temperature decreases (while remaining above 32° F [0° C]), the capacity of air to carry water in vapor form decreases. The dew point is the temperature at which the maximum vapor capacity of air is reached, and water starts to condense into liquid form. This diagram illustrates the dew point principle in air with high and low water contents. In air with a high water content, water remains in vapor form as the air cools from 30° to 25° C (86° to 77° F),

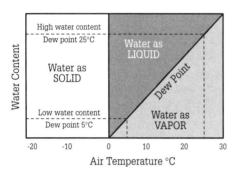

when the dew point is reached and condensation starts. As the air continues to cool, more of the water condenses to liquid form. In air with a low water content, water remains in vapor form as air cools from 30° to 5°C (86° to 41° F), when the dew point is reached and condensation starts.

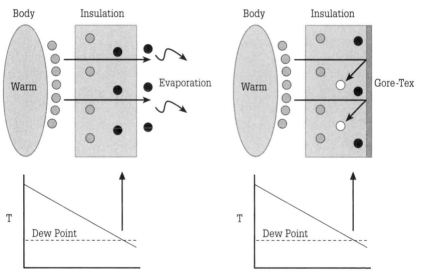

Figure 10-6. Temperature (T) decreases as water vapor (light circles) moves from a warm body, through clothing, to the exterior. When the air temperature falls below the dew point (dashed line), condensation occurs. If the liquid water (dark circles) can pass through the material, it evaporates with minimal water accumulation within the material (left panel). The right panel illustrates a potential problem with a liquid-resistant, vapor-permeable material, such as Gore-Tex, in extreme cold. If the dew point is reached within the clothing, the liquid water cannot escape through the liquid-resistant membrane and freezes (clear circles) within the clothing, adding weight and decreasing insulation.

According to this principle, if waterproof, breathable laminates are worn in very cold weather, they should only be worn as a single-layer outer shell, not as the surface layer of a thicker insulating garment so that ice crystals are not trapped within the garment. Elevating skin temperature also tends to drive the dew point farther from the body, increasing the probability that condensation occurs outside the clothing surface.

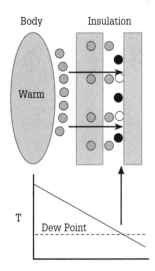

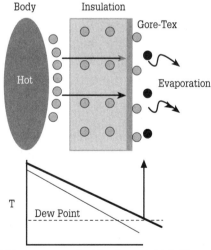

Figure 10-7. Some strategies to minimize moisture accumulation within clothing. Left panel above: *Layering increases the chance that the dew point is reached somewhere between clothing layers. If water vapor condenses and freezes between the layers, the ice can be brushed from the surfaces instead of being trapped within one of the layers.* Right panel, *above: Heavy work increases skin surface temperature and the dew point is reached outside of the clothing (heavy line) instead of within the material, as would have occurred with a lower initial skin temperature (light line).* Right panel: *An increased skin temperature is required to force water vapor through the liquid-resistant, vapor-permeable surface before it condenses and evaporates or freezes.*

CHAPTER 11

Left Out in the Cold:
Cold Weather Survival

MOST INDIVIDUALS do not plan to get into a survival situation when they leave their homes. That scenario develops when some adverse event makes a planned activity far more difficult than expected. The word survival is often misapplied. Situations may become difficult or inconvenient, but an argument can be made that the term should only be applied to situations in which surviving is actually in question.

Precipitating adverse events include: becoming lost while hiking or hunting; being stranded by vehicle breakdown or accident; illness; injury such as a fall while mountaineering; losing equipment, particularly clothing; accidents such as a snowmobile or skier falling through the ice; or being unexpectedly benighted by weather or an accident. Such events can occur in a variety of locations, ranging from close to home to isolated areas that include highways, cold or frozen bodies of water, woodland trails, or mountain slopes.

THE RULE OF 3'S

HUMANS CAN SURVIVE:
- ○ 3 minutes without air
- ○ 3 hours without heat
- ○ 3 days without water
- ○ 3 weeks without food

Three principle elements determine whether a precipitating event produces merely inconvenience or becomes a life-threatening event. With the required skills, proper equipment, and no major injury or illness, the experience may prove only difficult. However, with inadequate skills or equipment, or with significant injury or illness, the situation may rapidly deteriorate into a survival scenario.

A precipitating event often provides little or no warning of impending disaster. Often little, if any, time may be available for on-scene preparation, and only an individual's knowledge and experience and the equipment on hand can prevent disaster. This chapter describes the basics of preventing and preparing for survival, particularly in cold weather. Throughout, the overriding principle is to always prepare for the reasonable worst-case scenario.

PRIORITIES IN A SURVIVAL SITUATION

The body's physiological tolerances must be understood and preparations must have been made to have at hand whatever is required to facilitate rescue, either by one's self or by others. Clearly a person without oxygen as the result of drowning, choking, or a heart attack must be resuscitated immediately. After dealing with such emergencies, however, the physiological order of priority is heat, water, and food. Equipment can help individuals await rescue, get to safety through their own efforts, or signal rescuers. Anyone preparing for an outdoor activity in cold conditions should carry equipment and supplies that fall into the following five categories, listed in order of usual preference:

- ○ Fire
- ○ Shelter
- ○ Signals
- ○ Water
- ○ Food

In preparing for survival, attention should be paid not only to having the correct gear but also to not losing it during an adverse event. The most basic gear should always be carried in the pockets so it is always available. More sophisticated and bulky equipment can be carried in backpacks or in vehicles. As much as possible, items should be small, reliable, easily accessed, simple to use, and idiot proof.

SIMPLE WINTER SURVIVAL ITEMS (MINIMUM REQUIREMENTS)

CARRIED ON THE PERSON (POCKETS)
Lighter, matches, or flint match
Firestarter (cotton in Vaseline)
Whistle
Compass
Thick foil or other container for melting snow
High-energy food

CARRIED SEPARATELY (BACKPACK)
Lighter, matches, or flint match
Metal container for melting snow (may be kit container)
Jackknife
Shelter, plastic sheet (10 ft. x 10 ft., 3 m x 3 m)
Strong string or thin rope
Signal(s) such as pen flares, smoke flares, mirror
High-energy food

Fire

The ability to light a fire is arguably the most important winter survival skill in most areas of North America below the tree line. Except in extremely wet conditions, such as sleet or driving rain, a person can live for extended periods of time in relative comfort beside a good fire without an elaborate shelter. Fire provides heat and dries clothing, making the clothing more comfortable and maximizing its insulation value. Fire can be used to convert snow into drinking water or to disinfect water from lakes and rivers. It can also be used for cooking and provides a psychological boost during the potentially long wait for rescue. Finally, the smoke from a fire can provide an effective signal.

Two different methods for starting a fire should always be packed, and they should be carried in different locations in the clothing or backpack. A lighter is very efficient, but like all mechanical devices could fail due to a fuel leak or an ineffective flint and should not be relied on as the sole firestarter. Matches should be kept in a waterproof container and checked regularly. The sulfur ends often soften and become ineffective. Metal matches (also known as flint matches) reliably produce large sparks that easily light prepared firestarters (see below) and, with practice, can even light tinder. One type of metal match is Strike Force.

All outdoor enthusiasts should be well versed in fire building. Procedures are available in outdoor instructional texts, but one extremely valuable fire-starting aid is cotton balls (not synthetic facsimiles) impregnated with petroleum jelly (Vaseline), which produce a bomb-proof firestarter (Figure 11-1). After surface strands of cotton are teased away from the main ball—creating angel hair—a flame or spark easily ignites the cotton ball, which burns strongly for one to two minutes, providing plenty of time to ignite tinder or kindling. These balls light reliably even when wet. Of course, as with any fire-building method, proper preparation by collecting and organizing enough tinder, kindling, and firewood to create an effective fire is essential.

Shelter

Shelters provide protection from wind, rain, sleet, or snow. Many types exist. They can be made from materials included in survival kits or in camping gear. They can also be constructed from natural sources such as tree branches or snow (Figure 11-2). Finally, shelters can be fashioned from natural structures such as trees or rock outcroppings.

In a cold climate temporary shelters, including tents, must provide protection from the convective cooling of wind. Tents are not completely windproof. In extremely high winds most tents require some kind of windbreak to preserve structural integrity. Snow shelters, such as snow caves, hollowed mounds of snow (quinzees), and igloos, are much more effective than tents but require time, energy, and effective tools to construct. Other emergency

Figure 11-1. Bomb-proof firestarter. The surface fibers of cotton balls—real, not synthetic—impregnated with Vaseline, are teased away to produce angel hair. A flame, or even a spark with a flint match, easily ignites the cotton ball, which burns for up to two minutes. Five prepared cotton balls in a small plastic bag is a simple, economic "survival" package that should be placed in the pockets of clothing worn during wilderness experiences.

Figure 11-2. One example of an emergency shelter created from natural resources: a lean-to with evergreen branches.

shelters include a simple hole or trench dug in the snow and covered with a tarp, tent, or tree limbs. Such shelters block the wind and eliminate severe convective cooling. Additionally, since the air inside is relatively stationary, it can be warmed by heat from the body and provide a much more comfortable environment. If a large cave or hole is dug where wood is available, a fire can be built near the entrance to provide warmth.

Shelter should also provide protection from moisture and conductive cooling. At temperatures below freezing the moisture in exhaled air tends to form frost on the walls of tents or snow structures that can drop down on the occupants. This frost may be melted by body heat and dampen the outer surface of the sleeping bags. Frost accumulation within shelters is difficult to prevent and can be limited only by decreasing water vapor within the shelter. Steam must not be allowed to enter the tent during cooking. Frost buildup is decreased if occupants wear heat-moisture exchanging masks, or just place a scarf over the mouth while sleeping. Under no circumstances, however, should sleepers put their faces inside their sleeping bags during the night. All of the water vapor in the expired air enters the sleeping bag, usually condenses, and is trapped inside the bag.

When building show shelters, rounding the ceiling helps snowmelt run down the surface instead of dripping on anyone below. These structures breathe adequately for the first few days. After that, a thin layer of ice forms on the inner surface, decreasing breathability, and the snow becomes compact, reducing its insulation value.

When sitting or lying on snow, insulation is essential. An insulated sleeping pad is best; other equipment such as a backpack, climbing rope, tarp, or similar waterproof material, is better than nothing.

Building shelters and maintaining fires takes a significant amount of work, and a decision to prepare for an unexpected overnight stay usually must be made by early afternoon at the latest. These tasks are completed much more easily in daylight than at night.

Signals

The best way to succeed in a survival situation is to shorten it by signaling a search and rescue party. Signals must be simple, clear, and easily recognized. They can be audible, such as whistles or horns; visual, such as fires, flares, contrasting colors, or signal mirrors (Figure 11-3); or electronic, such as an emergency locating transmitter (ELT), cellular telephone, or satellite telephone. However, cellular telephones are useless if an emergency occurs in an out-of-service location.

Opposite: *Figure 11-3. Visual signals: signal mirror, smoke flare, and pyrotechnic flare*

Immersed individuals can increase visibility to airborne searchers by lying on their backs and kicking their legs vigorously. Two or more individuals should link arms to make a more visible formation.

Water and Food

Water and food support and fuel physiologic functions, maintain physical condition and mental acuity, and help prevent local cold injury and hypothermia. Water is most important. Without water, a person can die within a day in hot, dry climates and within three days in cold climates, although several individuals have survived as long as eight days after being trapped in vehicles or earthquake debris. Failure to replace normal water losses through the kidneys, skin, and lungs, or abnormal losses by other routes, results in dehydration, decreased blood volume, and in a cold environment impaired heat production by exercise. Dehydration is typically accompanied by weakness, fatigue, dizziness, and even a tendency to faint when standing, all of which impede efforts to deal rationally with a threatening environment.

Dehydration also contributes to other problems. Constriction of peripheral blood vessels increases the risk of frostbite. Shock may develop following relatively minor injuries. Clots tend to form in the legs and may result in pulmonary embolism, even though, in severely hypothermic individuals, the coagulation cascade is impaired.

In a dehydrated state the sensation of thirst is diminished or absent, and a conscious effort to consume adequate fluids must be made. Water intake with mild exertion should be at least two liters a day. With heavier exertion or at high altitude, three to five liters are required. In a world of snow and ice, fuel is required to melt snow for drinking water. Eating snow does not provide an adequate volume of water. However, the old adage "eating cold snow lowers body core temperature" is probably overstated. In an extreme thirst situation, placing some snow in the mouth provides only temporary relief, but does not present a significant thermal risk.

Melting snow for drinking water requires one essential utensil—a container. Survival kits and packs should include a container that can hold water; a metal cup, for example, can actually house the survival kit. A twelve-inch square of metal foil can be folded, placed in a jacket pocket, and used as an improvised container. This solultion is very compact, but care must be taken to prevent ripping the delicate foil.

An adequate fluid intake is indicated by urine that has a light yellow color and a volume of at least one liter every twenty-four hours. Obviously, actual urine volume measurement is unlikely, but individuals should be able to appreciate a reduced frequency for voiding, particularly the absence of a need to void after a night's sleep. They certainly can recognize the deep yellow or orange color of concentrated urine that is indicative of dehydration. When voiding into snow, orange "snow flowers" are an ominous sign.

Death from starvation takes far longer than death from dehydration, but food is needed for physical activity and heat production. Eating small amounts of food at frequent intervals helps prevent depletion of energy stores during the day. Some individuals with extensive outdoor experience seem to be munching almost continuously on mixtures of nuts, dried fruits, candies, and other high calorie food. Such mixtures are sold as gorp or trail mix or can be formulated individually at grocery store bulk-food sections.

In a survival situation, food is an important ingredient of success. Any source of food, even wild animals such as birds or rodents—which may have to be eaten uncooked—may be preferable to the fatigue, depression, and risk of cold injury that result from not eating.

PREPARATION

Prior to any outdoor activity, participants should consider the adage, "always prepare for the reasonable worst case scenario." They must practice skills such as navigation, survival tasks, and first aid. Their equipment must include survival gear, which should be distributed between pockets and packs. Plans should be developed for injuries and emergency evacuations.

Before leaving, information about planned activities, locations, and schedules, as well as contact information for the appropriate emergency personnel, should be left with a reliable person—preferably a loved one—who is in a situation to notice if the group does not return on time, and to initiate search and rescue procedures.

PREVENTION

Identifying as many reasonable worst case scenarios as possible facilitates preventing many of them. Accident prevention has many aspects. Safe driving can help avoid vehicular accidents. In the wilderness, horseplay should be controlled and tolerance for it should decrease as individuals get farther from safety. Conservative actions can prevent severe mishaps, such as avalanche burial or trauma while mountaineering. Accidental cold water immersion can result from falling overboard when standing in a boat; when kayaks, canoes, or rafts are swamped in white water; or when boats are capsized by high waves or by improper loading. Immersion can also occur when cross-country skiers or snowmobiles and other vehicles break through ice while traveling on frozen bodies of water.

To avoid becoming lost, individuals should establish their initial location on a map and regularly monitor their progress. Although a global positioning system (GPS) is valuable, it can fail and should not be relied upon as the sole navigation tool; a compass should always be carried by every individual in the wilderness.

Equipment is commonly lost by leaving it behind at a camp or rest spot, having it fall into water or down slopes, having it blown away or burned, or storing it in a vehicle that is lost in an accident, such as a car or snowmobile falling through the ice. Care should be taken to prevent such losses as only the equipment that remains on hand after a misadventure is of value.

Proper Procedure

The most important response to an adverse event is to avoid panic. Rapid action may be required to extract oneself from a dangerous situation such as a fire, an avalanche, or submersion under ice. However, once imminent danger has been resolved, more time should be taken to make reasoned decisions. An acronym for the proper emergency response is STOP:

    S—Stop

    T—Think

    O—Observe

    P—Plan

Following this pattern greatly improves decision making. Two common survival situations are being lost and being stranded in a known location. Children should be taught to "hug a tree" if they become lost and wait for an adult to find them. However, adults who become lost or disorientated may be able to regain their bearings with the STOP principle. A person could safely take a limited amount of time—fifteen to thirty minutes—to rationally try to find a familiar landmark or trail. If the allotted time passes without success, attention should be shifted to preparation for an emergency campsite and awaiting rescue.

If a person is stranded in a known location, as can occur with a vehicle breakdown or accident, a decision must be made whether to stay or go. Considerations that must be included in this decision include distance to safety, terrain that must be covered, navigation requirements, time of day, fitness and health of the individual(s), equipment and supplies on hand, and the time before a search party could reasonably be expected to reach the area. This complicated decision should be addressed in a conservative manner. Distances can be deceiving and rate of progress easily overestimated. Much energy can be required to walk over rough or snow-covered terrain, and nightfall can come faster than expected, particularly in winter.

If a decision is made to go, a cutoff time of early afternoon should be set. Much time, effort, and skill are required to construct an emergency campsite and build a fire. Preparing a shelter and collecting firewood is much easier during the day. If safety is not absolutely within reach by early afternoon, preparations should be made for an emergency camp.

COLD WATER IMMERSION

Special attention is required if an individual falls into very cold water, or through the ice. The brain is the most important survival tool; decisions often determine whether a person survives. Care must also be taken to protect the hands, the next most important survival tool, from freezing, otherwise the other survival decisions may be very difficult, or impossible to complete. With continued cooling in cold weather or cold water, the hands become less effective until they are useless. Progression to frostbite occurs in some situations.

Action steps:

o   If immersed in water, hands should be kept out of the water as much as possible. Water should be exited using the "kick and pull method."

o   Once out of the water, water should be wrung out of mittens, which should be kept on as much as possible; hands must not be allowed to freeze.

o   Unless it is bitterly cold, wet clothes should be removed and the water quickly wrung out, which makes a significant improvement in insulation and comfort until clothes can be dried over a fire. If it is too cold, however, clothing will freeze solid and become useless. The situation can be monitored by wringing water out of one piece of clothing at a time.

o   Numbness must never be accepted. In the cold, sensations progress from feelings of cold, to pain, numbness, and finally nothing. Absence of sensation occurs because the nerves are too cold to conduct impulses and the tissue is about to freeze.

o   Hands must be protected at all costs. If necessary, they can be placed in the armpits. Arms can be pulled inside a jacket so the hands can have direct contact with the armpits. Saving feet from frostbite may be impossible, but frostbite of the hands can be prevented in almost all situations, unless hands must be used constantly.

CHAPTER 12

Get Me Outta Here:
Ice Water Escape and Rescue

JUST BEFORE CHRISTMAS 1992, two couples were snowmobiling home from a bar late at night. The temperature was -4° F (-20° C) and heavy ice fog reduced visibility. The couples drove onto a frozen sewage lagoon and both machines broke through the ice. One couple escaped and called for help, but the other remained stranded in ice water that was seven to eight feet deep.

Twenty minutes elapsed before a rescue call was put in and local police arrived at the scene. At this time the female was floating face down in the water and the male was in open water about ten feet from the edge of the ice with his head and shoulders slightly raised above the surface. He probably was standing on his submerged snowmobile. The police had no special training or equipment for ice water rescue, but one member ventured out on the ice and became stranded as the ice broke up around him. Two other constables found an aluminum boat on shore and started walking it toward the victim. When the ice broke they were forced into the boat only to find out that it had several holes in the floor and was taking on enough water to sink.

After twenty-five minutes in the water, the male victim suddenly slumped forward and drowned. Another thirty minutes elapsed before the fire department arrived and rope-secured personnel were able to bring the three stranded "rescuers" to safety, and transport them to a hospital for treatment for cold exposure. The drowned victims were recovered by a dive team about two hours later.

This accident exemplifies several features of cold water immersion. After twenty-five minutes of immersion in ice water, the male, who was of medium build, probably was only mildly hypothermic when he drowned. He very likely could have survived another hour or more if his airway had been supported above water after he lost consciousness. By the time emergency personnel arrived, this individual was no longer experiencing cold shock and was becoming incapacitated by cold. If the rescuers had been familiar with cold water physiology, they would have realized that he could survive in ice water much longer than most people think.

With this in mind, the victim needed to be coaxed to the ice edge, to place his arms on the ice, and to remain motionless. The ice would have supported his weight and he would not have needed to struggle. Once his arms were frozen to the ice, he would be protected from drowning and could survive for a considerable time until his heart became cold enough to stop, which might have taken two or more hours.

The absolute necessity for rescue personnel not to become secondary victims during a rescue attempt must be emphasized. Bystanders and rescue personnel often get caught up in the moment and rush in to save someone in trouble. Thankfully, none of these professionals were lost. They were lucky, unlike others described in news headlines such as these:

"Search Continues for 3 Teens, Adults Who Tried to Save Them"

"Volunteer Firefighter Died a Hero in Rescue Try"

"Girl Dies Trying to Save Dog in Frozen Pond"

"Couple Drown in Attempt to Save Dog"

"Three Teens Perish in New York State Trying to Pull Doomed Friend from River"

"Christian School Worker Drowns Trying to Remove Boy from Lake"

"U.S. Air Force Sergeant Drowns in Rescue off Bermuda's Coast"

This chapter describes the processes that should be followed for escape and rescue from ice-cold water. The principles of self-rescue are followed by rescue principles for bystanders and trained personnel.

SELF-RESCUE

Most people have a poor understanding of how their body reacts during ice water immersion. The following principles are based on the easy-to-remember slogan "One Minute—Ten Minutes—One Hour." Although individuals vary in the timing of events, the principles apply to everyone.

One minute to get breathing under control. Uninformed people think they can die of hypothermia within only a few minutes of ice water immersion, and tend to panic, which must be avoided. The first priority is to get breathing under control so that gasping and hyperventilation do not result in gulping water or even drowning. Slow deep breaths are best.

Ten minutes of meaningful movement. Once breathing is under control, an individual must try to get out of ice water as quickly as possible, usually needing a burst of energy to do so. In cold water, loss of arm control and loss of the ability to grasp is progressive, and this deficit is substantial within the first ten minutes. The person should take time to determine where the ice is most likely to hold the body's weight, which is usually near the point of immersion. After putting arms up on the ice, the individual should keep the face close to the ice to keep the upper body low (kiss the ice), kick the legs until the body is horizontal, then kick vigorously and pull the body up onto the ice. Once on the ice, the person must roll away from the hole, and not stand up. If the person is close to the shore, it may be possible to roll all the way to shore.

If the incident occurred farther from shore, the individual should not stand up until the ice is thick enough to support the weight.

When safely away from the hole, the individual must immediately work to get water out of clothing and make a decision whether to go to safety or prepare to stay and wait for rescue.

One hour before becoming unconscious due to hypothermia. If individuals cannot get out of the ice-cold water within ten to fifteen minutes they must recognize that, although they might not yet be hypothermic, physical incapacitation continually gets worse. Although self-rescue may no longer be possible, the individual can still remain conscious for an hour or more. Appropriate action must be taken to extend survival time and widen the window of opportunity for rescue.

Individuals should place their arms on the ice and lay their heads on their arms to reduce the chance of sliding backwards in to the water if their heads should fall backward. They must stop struggling, as this only increases heat loss and quickly results in exhaustion. The arms may freeze to the ice, which would keep the person's airway above water if consciousness is lost. In more temperate conditions—such as during spring break-up—arms may not freeze to the ice, but minimizing movement should still prevail.

If an immersed individual is wearing a snowmobile helmet and it can be taken off easily, it can provide up to twelve pounds of buoyancy, almost as much as a certified personal flotation device (PDF).

Clothing should be kept on while in the water, as clothes help conserve body heat, and the air trapped inside initially provides buoyancy. Water eventually replaces the trapped air, but wet clothing does not pull an individual down. Even though up to eighty pounds (36 kg) of water can be absorbed by the clothing, this water has the same density as water outside the clothing and does not pull the victim beneath the surface. The water in the suit does have significant inertia, making it difficult to move arms and legs in the water, but the greatest difficulty with water in clothing is encountered during exit when the weight must be raised above the water surface.

RESCUING OTHERS

Untrained bystanders should be very careful and use common sense. Trained rescue personnel must follow guidelines established by their service. The Toronto Police Marine Unit offers an extensive ice rescue course, and their philosophy of ice-water rescue is described below. Anyone attempting a rescue should:

Consider safety of:
○ Rescuer(s)
○ Others (victim's friends and bystanders)
○ Only then . . . the victim

Assess:

○ Victim's condition
○ Ice or water condition
○ Equipment and manpower available

Consider low-risk methods first, then higher risk methods

The first priority for bystanders is to contact emergency personnel but they must also note the spot where the individual went through the ice. (They can mark the spot from several spots on shore and pick landmarks on the other side of the water that line up with the person.) Rescuers may later make holes during rescue efforts and the "last seen point" may be lost, making recovery difficult if the subject drowns.

Untrained bystanders should only attempt low-risk methods that can be completed from shore or from some other safe location such as a dock. These methods are listed below according to increased difficulty and exposure.

Talk rescues: instructing and encouraging self-rescue. Immersed persons should be instructed not to panic and to get breathing under control by taking deep slow breaths while moving to the ice edge and getting their arms up on the ice as far as possible. The individuals should then be guided through the "kick and pull" self-rescue procedure. If self-rescue is not successful, subjects should be informed that they can survive for an extended period of time if their arms are placed on the ice and they remain motionless. If the ice is unstable and continues to break, or bends and sinks beneath the water surface, the individuals can be instructed to gather small sheets of ice and place them underneath the ice edge, which may effectively increase ice thickness and make the supporting ice edge stronger, more buoyant, and stable.

Throw rescues: throwing buoyant objects or ropes to a victim. If a rope is used, the rescuer should tie a loop in the end of the rope by folding the last three feet (one meter) of rope on itself and tying an overhand knot where the free end meets the main rope. The person should be instructed to either place the loop over the head and under the arms, or to place one arm through the loop and hook the elbow through the rope. Alternatively, the subject can be instructed to wrap the rope around the forearm a few times, which requires less strength and dexterity to hold on to the rope.

All rescue groups should have commercial throw bags with a minimum of fifty feet of rope, which can be purchased at any boating equipment store at a reasonable price. All private and professional vehicles that travel on the ice (snowmobiles, all-terrain vehicles, cars, trucks) should have a throw bag easily accessible for rapid deployment (Figure J in color insert).

Reach rescues: extending a long object such as a ladder or tree branch to a victim. Rescuers should follow the procedure outlined for "throw" rescues.

Trained rescue personnel should first attempt the low-risk methods listed above. If these are not successful they may attempt higher risk methods, which are classified as "Platform-assisted" and "Go" rescues.

All rescue personnel should be properly equipped before stepping out on the ice. The minimum personal gear includes an insulated dry suit and helmet, a personal flotation device, a harness for attachment to a security rope, ice picks, and a whistle.

Rescuers should always be attached to a security rope that is belayed from shore. Assistants on shore must realize that when the entire water surface is not frozen, shore ice slabs can release and break into smaller pieces, putting anyone standing on them at risk (Figure 12-1).

Examples of rescue gear include a flotation sling and sled, which may be used separately or together (Figure K in color insert). The sling is placed under the victim's arms and provides some flotation as well as creating a harness for pulling the victim out of the water.

Platform-assisted rescues: using some type of movable platform to transport a victim through broken ice or over solid ice (Figure 12-2). The preferred rescue method involves the use of some type of movable platform. Such platforms are available commercially (flotation sleds or inflatable boats) (Figure 12-3), or may be found in the area (fishing boats; a canoe is not an acceptable rescue platform).

Go rescues: approaching the victim with minimal rescue equipment. Go rescues should only be attempted if the rescuer is wearing insulated flotation gear, is harnessed and tied into a rope, and no rescue platform is available. The rescuer approaches by walking on the ice or wading and swimming through broken ice; if at all possible the rescuer should carry a rescue sling or some other nonplatform type of rescue aid.

IMPORTANCE OF TEAMWORK BETWEEN RESCUERS

Whether rescuers are trained or untrained they must remain calm so they can make the decisions necessary to allow the victim to survive longer and the rescuers to work safely and effectively as a team. Professional rescue personnel should regularly practice in conditions that are as realistic as can be safely achieved. Each training exercise should include all aspects of an expected rescue, not only extraction of the victim from the water, but treatment for injuries, and delivery to a transport vehicle.

Practice/training sessions should allow individuals to:

○ Set clear goals, responsibilities, and expectations
○ Effectively communicate
○ Learn their responsibilities and those of others
○ Coordinate efforts
○ Keep the "team," not the "individual," in mind

Figure 12-1. Example of how ice can break up and float away from shore. When these "victim demonstrators" first went on the ice, it was in one piece and attached to the shore. The ice soon broke up and the wind blew the men into open water.

Figure 12-2. Platform-based rescue. Victim is secured on rescue board with the flotation sling. Rescuer is attached to the board and drags behind the victim.

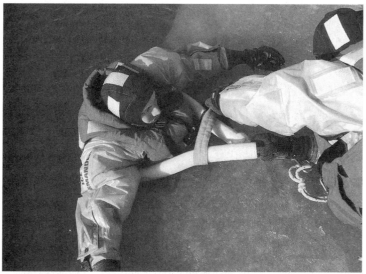

Figure 12-3. Inflatable boat (Fortuna) has no deck in the front and back, allowing rescuers to walk the boat over solid ice or paddle it on open water. These openings also allow a victim to be pulled directly onto the boat deck for transport.

Field operations should also be held during which individuals:
○ Execute planned protocols
○ Follow and practice leadership
○ Communicate effectively
○ Learn personnel, equipment, and knowledge requirements

SPECIAL COLD WATER CONSIDERATION: ESCAPE FROM A SINKING VEHICLE

Road vehicles are commonly driven onto the ice, either on established ice roads or directly to locations such as ice fishing areas. Every year in North America about four hundred individuals die in submersed vehicles, many of which have broken through ice.

A passenger vehicle (car, truck, or van) undergoes three phases after it breaks through the ice (Figure L in color insert).

Floating

Initially, a vehicle floats for thirty seconds to two minutes before the water reaches the level of the side windows, which provides ample time to get out of the vehicle. During this phase windows can easily be opened and used as exits. The doors should not be opened because this allows rapid influx of water and could cause the vehicle to submerge very quickly—within seconds—and water pressure may slam the door on anyone trying to get out. Exiting through an open window is relatively easy. Even electric windows should open as they are designed to work for a few minutes even when completely submerged.

A vehicle often partially breaks through the ice and rests on the surface for a short period. This is the only situation in which the door may be opened. Occupants should get out immediately and not linger near the vehicle. If the door is shut when the vehicle breaks through the ice and starts sinking, it should not be opened and people should always exit through the window.

Sinking

The sinking phase extends from the time when the water rises above the bottom of the side windows to when the vehicle is completely under water, but before the inside fills completely with water, allowing the occupants to breathe. During this period water is rising inside the vehicle, but the water level outside is higher, which exerts pressure against the doors and windows, making them very difficult or impossible to open. As the vehicle fills with water, it tilts heavy/engine-end down (usually forward) into an almost vertical position. Normally, all the air escapes through the trunk; but if the water is shallower than fifteen feet (five meters) the vehicle many land right side up and some air may be trapped in the upper portion of the interior. However, the chances for escape and survival decrease considerably during this phase and occupants should not rely on an air pocket.

Submerged

The vehicle is full of water and no air pockets exist. This can occur either before or after the vehicle lands on the bottom, depending on the water depth. If the water is deeper than fifteen to twenty feet (five to seven meters) the vehicle typically pitches forward enough to end up inverted and on its roof. If the vehicle is full of water and on the bottom, the chance of survival is negligible.

Clearly, the best time to escape from a vehicle that has broken through the ice is during the initial floating phase. Cold shock is much better dealt with after exiting the vehicle, than while trapped inside during the sinking phase.

The following escape procedure should be followed:

Unfasten Seatbelts: Everyone should immediately insure that seatbelts are unfastened.

Secure Children: If children are in the car, their seatbelts should be unfastened and they should be brought close to an adult who can assist in their escape.

Open Windows: Windows should be rolled down as quickly as possible. If water has risen above the front side windows, individuals can move to the rear seat and roll down the rear windows. If moving to the back is not possible, every effort should be made to open the front window even if water starts to pour in (see below).

Get Out: Children should be pushed out of the window first, and followed immediately. If two or more vehicle occupants are old enough to exit the vehicle themselves, they should each use the window closest to them. Some rear windows are child-proofed and cannot be opened enough for escape and rear-seat occupants must quickly follow front-seat occupants out the front windows. The writer conducted demonstrations during which four adults and a child mannequin released from a child seat in the rear were able to exit through a single window (driver's side) within forty seconds.

If for some reason the vehicle cannot be exited before entering the sinking phase, every effort must be made to open the windows. No advantage is gained by waiting until the vehicle lands on the bottom; in virtually all instances the deeper the vehicle submerges, the less the chance of survival. If these efforts fail, and the occupants have survived until the vehicle is almost full of water, they may be able to open a door and exit.

Once out of the vehicle, individuals should look upward immediately to ensure they are moving toward the point of entry or other opening in the ice. Looking up also helps avoid hitting any heavy objects that are floating on the water surface. After reaching the surface, the "kick and pull" self-rescue technique should be used to get out on the ice.

DRIVING ON ICE

Clearly the best strategy to prevent a drowning from vehicle submersion is to avoid driving on the ice at all times. However, if a vehicle is going to be driven on the ice, efforts should be made to minimize the possibility of breaking through by driving only on ice roads officially opened by authorities (winter roads), or on ice known to be at least eight to twelve inches (twenty to thirty cm) thick (Figure 12-4).

Even when the ice has been deemed "safe," occupants should be prepared for breaking through:

- The escape procedure outlined above should be mentally rehearsed (transport of small children in vehicles on uncontrolled ice routes should be avoided).
- One life jacket, or PFD, should be available for each person in the vehicle (preferably worn rather than carried).
- Seatbelts should be unfastened at all times when driving on ice.
- An implement to break a window, such as a center punch or hammer, is advisable and should be in plain view with easy access,

preferably on the dashboard. (No time to search for it is available if the vehicle breaks through the ice.)

○ Windows may also be rolled down, particularly if electrically powered.

○ If an individual is inadvertently in a situation in which ice thickness is questionable, driving with the door open may be advantageous. If the vehicle breaks through the ice, the open door allows immediate exit and might come to rest against unbroken ice, slowing submersion of the vehicle.

Heavy machinery and trucks are often used in preparation and maintenance of winter roads and for transport. These vehicles do not float like passenger vehicles and may sink completely below the surface in as little as three seconds. This situation is very hazardous and the escape protocol is much less likely to be successful. An important preparation measure is the installation of a commercial escape hatch in the roof of the cab. Of course, an even better measure is to confirm a safe ice thickness before driving on it.

Figure 12-4. Recommended minimum ice thickness for different activities and weights. Values refer to new, clear, hard ice.

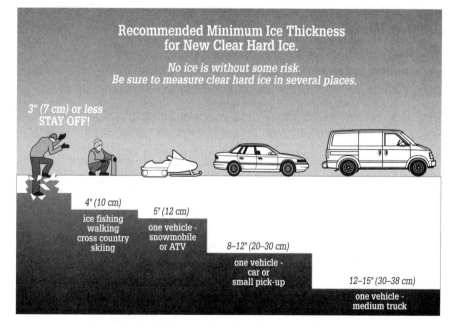

GLOSSARY

acidosis – A condition in which the pH of the blood is decreased or more acidic, a typical finding with moderate to severe hypothermia.

alkalosis – A condition in which the pH of the blood is increased or more alkaline, commonly the result of hyperventilation.

asystole – Totally absent heartbeat.

ataxia – Lacking the ability to coordinate muscle function.

atrial fibrillation – A condition in which the normal rhythmical contractions of the cardiac atria are replaced by rapid irregular twitchings that cause the ventricles to beat irregularly; commonly associated with decreased cardiac function.

bolus – A single, relatively large quantity of a substance, such as a drug intended for therapeutic use, taken orally or administered intravenously.

cardiac output – The amount of blood pumped by the heart in a specific time period.

core – The central or core tissues of the body, generally considered to consist of the heart, lungs, liver, and brain.

distal – More remote or at a greater distance from the center of the body.

dysrhythmia – An abnormal cardiac rhythm.

frostbite – A localized cold injury characterized by freezing of the tissues.

homeostasis – The ability of the body to maintain internal equilibrium by adjusting its physiological processes under fluctuating environmental conditions.

hyperventilation – An increased rate and depth of breathing.

hypocarbia – A condition in which the carbon dioxide concentration in the blood is lower than normal.

hypothermia – A lower than normal body temperature.

hypoxia – A condition in which the oxygen concentration, particularly the oxygen concentration in the blood or body tissues, is lower than normally found at sea level.

intravenous – Within or administered into a vein; a technique for administering drugs or fluids.

IV – Common abbreviation for intravenous.

lesion – A localized abnormality in a body organ or tissue.

normothermia – A normal body temperature.

periphery – The peripheral tissues of the body, generally considered to consist of the skin and subcutaneous fat of the trunk and all of the tissues of the arms and legs.

proximal – Nearer the central part of the body.

vasoconstriction – Blood vessel constriction.

vasodilatation – Dilatation of blood vessels.

ventricular fibrillation – An often lethal condition characterized by irregular, uncoordinated contractions of the muscle fibers of the heart instead of normal synchronous contractions in which the pumping action of the heart and effective cardiac function is lost.

SELECTED REFERENCES

CHAPTER FOUR

State of Alaska Cold Injuries Guidelines (www.chems.alaska.gov/EMS/Downloads_Rx.htm)

Danzl, D. F. "Accidental Hypothermia." In *Wilderness Medicine: Management of Wilderness and Environmental Emergencies*, 4th ed., edited by Paul S. Auerbach, 135–78. St. Louis: Mosby, 2001.

Danzl, D. F., and R. S. Pozos. "Accidental Hypothermia." *New England Journal of Medicine* 331 (1994): 1756–60.

Giesbrecht, G. G. "Cold Stress, Near Drowning and Accidental Hypothermia: A Review." *Aviation, Space and Environmental Medicine* 71 (2000): 733–52.

CHAPTER SEVEN

Fobson, M. C., and J. P. Heggers. "Evaluation of Hand Frostbite Blister Fluid as a Clue to Pathogensis." *Journal of Hand Surgery* 6 (1981): 43-47.

McCauley, R. I., D. N. Hing, M. C. Robson, and J. P. Heggers. "Frostbite Injuries: A Rational Approach Based on the Pathophysiology." *Journal of Trauma* 23 (1983): 143–47.

Sumner, D. S., T. L. Criblez, and W. H. Doolittle. "Host Factors in Human Frostbite." *Military Medicine* 139 (1974): 454–61.

CHAPTER EIGHT

Akers, W. A. "Paddy Foot: A Warm Water Immersion Foot Syndrome Variant." *Military Medicine* 139 (1974): 605–18.

Marsh, A. R. "A Short But Distant War—The Falklands Campaign." *Journal of the Royal Society of Medicine* 76 (1983): 972–82.

CHAPTER NINE

Anderson, S. D., R. E. Schoeffel, J. L. Black, and E. Daviskas. "Airway Cooling as the Stimulus to Exercise-induced Asthma: A Re-evaluation." *European Journal of Respiratory Disease* 67 (1985): 20–30.

Bonadonna, P., S. Gianenrico, and P. Zanon, et al. "Cold Induced Rhinitis in Skiers—Clinical Aspects and Treatment with Ipratroium Bromide Nasal Spray: A Randomized Controlled Trial." *American Journal of Radiology* 15 (2001): 297–301.

Burgess, K. R., and W. A. Whitelaw. "Reducing Ventilatory Response to Carbon Dioxide by Breathing Cold Air." *American Review of Respiratory Disease* 129 (1984): 687–90.

Coleridge, H. M., and J. C. G. Coleridge. "Reflexes Evoked from Tracheobronchial Tree and Lungs." In *Handbook of Physiology: The Respiratory System, Control of Breathing*, edited by N. S. Cherniack and J. G. Widdicombe, 395–424. Bethesda, Md.: American Physiological Society, 1986.

Coskey, R. J., and A. H. Mehregan. "Shoe Boot Pernio." *Archives of Dermatology* 109 (1974): 56–57.

Crowson, A. N., and C. M. Magro. "Idiopathic Perniosis and Its Mimics: A Clinical and Histological Study of 38 Cases." *Human Pathology* 28, no. 4 (1997): 478–84.

Duncan, W. C., R. G. Freeman, and C. L. Heaton. "Cold Panniculitis." *Archives of Dermatology* 94 (1966): 722–24.

Giesbrecht, G. G. "The Respiratory System in a Cold Environment." *Aviation, Space and Environmental Medicine* 66 (1995): 890–902.

Goette, D. L. "Chilblains (Perniosis)." *Academic Dermatology* 23 (1990): 257–62.

Haas, N., E. Toppe, and B.M. Henz. "Microscopic Morphology of Different Types of Urticaria." *Archives of Dermatology* 134 (1998): 41–46.

Inoue, G., and T. Miura. "Microgeodic Disease Affecting the Hands and Feet of Children." *Journal of Pediatric Orthopedics* 11, no. 1 (1991): 59–63.

Josenhans, W. T., G. N. Melville, and W. T. Ulmer. "The Effect of Facial Cold Stimulation on Airway Conductance in Healthy Men." *Canadian Journal of Physiology and Pharmacology* 47 (1969): 453–57.

Lowe, L. B. "Cold Panniculitis in Children." *American Journal of Diseases of Children* 115 (1968): 709–13.

Mann, T. P., and R. K. Elliott. "Neonatal Cold Injury Due to Accidental Exposure to the Cold." *Lancet* 1 (1957): 229–34.

Mathelier-Fusade, P. "Clinical Predictive Factors of Severity in Cold Urticaria." *Archives of Dermatology* 134 (1998): 106–7.

Numata, T., A. Konno, and S. Hasegawa, et al. "Pathophysiological Nasal Features in Patients with Idiopathic Rhinitis Compared to Allergic Rhinitis." *International Archives of Allergy and Immunology* 119 (1999): 304–13.

Pierson, W. E., and R. O. Voy. "Exercise-induced Bronchospasm in Winter Sports." In *Winter Sports Medicine*, edited by M. J. Casey, C. Foster, and E. G. Hixson, 158–66. Philadelphia: F. A. Davis Company, 1990.

Rajkumar, S. V., T. A. Laude, R. M. Russo, and V. J. Gururaj. "Popsicle Panniculitis of the Cheeks: A Diagnostic Entity Caused by Sucking on Cold Objects." *Clinical Pediatrics* (1976): 619–21.

Rotman, H. "Cold Panniculitis in Children—Case Reports." *Archives of Dermatology* 94 (1966): 620–651.

Strauss, R. H., E. R. McFadden, Jr., and R. H. Ingram, Jr., et al. "Enhancement of Exercise-induced Asthma by Cold Air." *New England Journal of Medicine* 297 (1977): 743–47.

Weston, W. W., and J. G. Morelli. "Childhood Pernio and Cryoproteins." *Pediatric Dermatology* 17, no. 2 (2000): 97–99.

INDEX

ABOUT THE AUTHORS

GORDON GIESBRECHT, PH.D. is a professor of thermophysiology at the University of Manitoba in Winnipeg, Canada where he runs the Laboratory for Exercise and Environmental Medicine and studies human responses to exercise and work in extreme environments. Gordon combines practical experience as a wilderness instructor with 20 years of human cold research. He has conducted hundreds of laboratory and field trials, which have led to publication of more than 100 articles about cold physiology and pre-hospital care for human hypothermia. He is a former board member of the Wilderness Medical Society.

Gordon Giesbrecht

Dubbed "Professor Popsicle" by *Outside magazine* and "Dr. Cool" by *Reader's Digest*, Gordon has been featured on the Discovery Channel, National Geographic Channel and various national television networks. Gordon has developed an effective strategy for educating the public and professionals alike about the risks and realities of cold. Through several media efforts, including an appearance on the "Late Show With David Letterman," Gordon has popularized effective slogans such as "1 minute – 10 minutes – 1 hour" for immersion in icy water, and "Seatbelts – Children – Windows – Out" about escaping from vehicles in water. Gordon's passion for research that makes a difference is stressed by his laboratory motto "Vitas Salvantes" which is Latin for "saving lives."

JIM WILKERSON is the editor of the first edition of *Hypothermia, Frostbite, and Other Cold Injuries*, which was originally published in 1986. He is also the editor of *Medicine for Mountaineering*, first published in 1967, and now in its fifth edition. Jim is a frequent lecturer at wilderness medical conferences and is the author or coauthor of more than sixty-five professional publications. An avid backpacker and climber, Jim has ascended Mount McKinley as well as peaks in Asia, Africa, and South America. He is also a whitewater rafter who has rafted the Grand Canyon several times; a scuba enthusiast who has caught and eaten more than his share of spiny lobsters; and a pilot who has owned acrobatic aircraft. Fifty years after entering medical school he retired from the practice of anatomic pathology in California, and now resides with his wife of forty-eight years in Park City, Utah, where they can ski forty to fifty days each season, and their home has enough bedrooms to insure that their four children, seven grandchildren, and many friends visit frequently.

Jim Wilkerson

THE MOUNTAINEERS, founded in 1906, is a nonprofit outdoor activity and conservation club, whose mission is "to explore, study, preserve, and enjoy the natural beauty of the outdoors . . . ." The club sponsors many classes and year-round outdoor activities in the Pacific Northwest, and supports environmental causes through educational activities, sponsoring legislation and presenting educational programs. The Mountaineers Books supports the club's mission by publishing travel and natural history guides, instructional texts, and works on conservation and history.

Send or call for our catalog of more than 500 outdoor titles:

The Mountaineers Books
1001 SW Klickitat Way, Suite 201
Seattle, WA 98134
800-553-4453
mbooks@mountaineersbooks.org
www.mountaineersbooks.org